SPECTRUM®
LANGUAGE ARTS

Grade 2

CREDITS
Editors: Jennifer B. Stith, Hailey Scragg
Cover Design: J.J. Giddings, Nick Pearson, Lynne Schwaner
Interior Design: Nick Pearson
Illustrations: Nick Pearson, Max Porter, J.J. Giddings, Josh Janes, Robin Krantz, Morgan Burnside

Spectrum®
An imprint of Carson Dellosa Education
PO Box 35665
Greensboro, NC 27425 USA

Printed in the USA • All rights reserved.
ISBN 978-1-4838-7136-3
01-057247784

Table of Contents Grade 2

Table of Contents Grade 2

Spectrum Introduction

For more than 20 years, Spectrum® workbooks have been the solution for helping students meet and exceed learning goals. Each title in the Spectrum workbook series offers grade-appropriate instruction and reinforcement in an effective sequence for learning success.

Spectrum partners with you in supporting your student's educational journey every step of the way! This book will help them navigate second grade language arts and will give you the support you need to make sure your student learns everything they need to know. Inside you will find:

Chapter Introductions

These introductions provide useful information about the chapter. Including:

Background Information
This introductory text provides you with background information about specific skills taught in the chapter.

Helpful Definitions
These terms either appear in the chapter or are important for the skills being taught.

Skills Checklist
This checklist helps ensure your student is practicing grade-level skills.

Tools and Tips
Tools and tips to support and reinforce skills are explained here.

Lessons

These pages begin with a definition, step-by-step instructions where needed, and examples, followed by independent practice.

Enrichment

These problems appear throughout the book. They allow your student to dig deeper and apply the skill they learned in a different way than it is practiced on the page. The two types of problems will ask your student to think critically and explain reasoning.

Chapter Reviews

These end-of-chapter reviews go over the skills learned within each chapter and can be used to gauge your student's progress.

Learning Checkpoints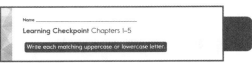

These reviews break up the book into halfway points to prepare your student for the final test.

Final Test

This test covers the skills learned in the book. Use this comprehensive test to assess what your student has learned and to identify what they still need to work on.

Answer Key

The answers to the lessons, reviews, and tests are provided in an answer key.

Chapter 1: Parts of Speech

We begin this *Spectrum Language Arts* book for Grade 2 with a focus on the parts of speech. Chapter 1 introduces students to nouns, pronouns, verbs, adjectives, and adverbs.

Students will learn how to identify the different types of nouns—common, proper, and collective—that they will come across while reading and will use in their writing. Learning to always capitalize a proper noun to identify it as an important name of a person, place, or thing is an important skill that helps with reading and writing.

Other important building blocks of sentences covered in this chapter are pronouns, including reflexive and indefinite pronouns. Students learn about how using pronouns in place of the same noun over and over again can give their writing a better flow and can be more fun for the reader. Verbs are necessary elements for complete sentences. While focusing on verbs, encourage learners to vary their verb choice to add some pizzazz to their writing.

Skills Checklist

☐ Identifying common and collective nouns

☐ Identifying proper nouns and using correct capitalization

☐ Identifying pronouns, including reflexive and indefinite pronouns

☐ Identifying and using verbs

☐ Identifying and using adjectives

☐ Identifying and using adverbs

common noun: a word that names a person, place, thing, or idea; usually not capitalized; Examples: *brother, library, lake*

collective noun: a noun that refers to a group of people, animals, or things; Examples: *flock* of sheep, *crowd* of people, *bouquet* of flowers

proper noun: a word that names a specific person, place, thing, or idea; begins with a capital letter; Examples: *Nintendo, Mount Everest, Jonas*

pronoun: a word that takes the place of a noun; Examples: *they, her, we, it*

reflexive pronoun: words ending in *-self* or *-selves*; Examples: *myself, itself, yourselves*

indefinite pronoun: a pronoun that doesn't specifically identify what it is referring to; Examples: *somebody, everything, nothing*

verb: an action word that tells what happens in a sentence; Examples: *jump, write, played*

adjective: a word that describes nouns or pronouns; Examples: *fluffy* cat, *red* bike, *scary* movie

adverb: a word that describes verbs, adjectives, and other adverbs; usually ends in *-ly*; Examples: I *quietly* read a book. The turtles *slowly* crossed the road.

Your best tool for reinforcing parts of speech might just be in your student's pencil box! By using different colors of crayon or pencil, students can highlight parts of speech in their writing or in others' writings. Encourage your student to circle, underline, and label their way to understanding each part of speech and its role in writing clear, concise, and interesting sentences.

For a more visual and kinesthetic activity that supports understanding the parts of speech, write parts of speech on different colors of index cards. Have your student move around the cards to build phrases and sentences.

Lesson 1.1 Common Nouns and Collective Nouns

A **common noun** is a word that names a person, place, or thing.

    brother (person)   **park** (place)   **bicycle** (thing)

A **collective noun** is a word for a group of animals, things, or people.

    a **herd** of horses   a **deck** of cards   a **troupe** of actors

Read the paragraph. Circle each common noun.

I packed my bag for camp. I packed shirts, pants,

socks, and shoes. I added my toothbrush and a comb.

My mom said to bring a hat. My dad said to bring a game

and a book. I wanted to bring my cat. My mom and

dad said cats do not go to camp. I brought a photo of my

cat, instead.

Can you write another sentence for the paragraph that uses a collective noun? Try it!

_____

_____

Name _____

Lesson 1.1 Common Nouns and Collective Nouns

Complete each sentence with a collective noun from the box.

| fleet | flock | litter | team | school | pod |

1. A _____ of birds landed in the apple tree.

2. Grace's cat gave birth to a _____ of six kittens.

3. The _____ of hockey players boarded the bus.

4. A _____ of ships left the harbor at noon.

5. The shark spotted a _____ of fish.

6. A _____ of dolphins leaped beside the boat.

 Explain why the word *school* is not always used as a collective noun.

_____

_____

Name _____

Lesson 1.2 Proper Nouns

A **proper noun** names a special person, place, or thing. Proper nouns begin with a capital letter to show that they are important.

Common Nouns		Proper Nouns
school	⟶	Cox Elementary School
sister	⟶	Isabella
city	⟶	Los Angeles
pet	⟶	Bailey

Read each sentence. Underline the nouns. Write the letter **C** above each common noun. Write the letter **P** above each proper noun.

1. The students in my class are going on a trip.

2. We are going to the New England Museum.

3. I am going to sit near Carson, Maddy, and Maria on the bus.

4. Mr. Cohen said that we will have lunch in the cafeteria.

5. My family and I visited a museum when we went to Chicago.

Can you list two proper nouns that are important to you? Try it!

_____

_____

Name _____

Lesson 1.2 Proper Nouns

> Read and proofread the paragraph. If a proper noun does not begin with a capital letter, underline the first letter three times. Then, write the capital letter above it.

Example: Max and enrique went to buxton Public Library after school.

Chicago is the largest city in illinois. It is near the shores of lake michigan.

Aunt suzanne lives there. My sister, ellie, loves to visit her in chicago. They like to

go to the museums. Uncle alex said I can come

visit next time.

Explain when you would capitalize nouns such as *library, school,* or *ocean.*

_____

_____

_____

Lesson 1.3 Pronouns

A **pronoun** is a word that takes the place of a noun. Some pronouns are: *I, me, you, he, she, him, her, it, we, us, they,* and *them.*

<u>Drew and Lei</u> play piano every day.
↓
They play piano every day.

Dad parked <u>the car</u> in the garage.
↓
Dad parked **it** in the garage.

> Read the paragraph. Circle the pronouns.

I will never forget the first soccer game I ever saw. Mom, Dad, Laura, and

I drove downtown to the stadium. It was lit up against the night sky. We were

excited to see the Rangers play. The stadium was filled with hundreds of people.

They cheered when the players ran onto the field. Laura and I screamed and

clapped. We laughed when the Rangers' mascot did a funny dance. The best part

of the game was when Matt Ramos scored the winning goal. He is the best player

on the team. It was a night to remember!

Name _____

Lesson 1.3 Pronouns

Read each pair of sentences. Write the correct pronoun to take the place of the underlined word or words.

1. Mom drove <u>Anna</u> to soccer practice.

   Mom drove _____ to soccer practice.
   (it, her)

2. <u>Dana and Marcia</u> are on Anna's team.

   _____ are on Anna's team.
   (Them, They)

3. <u>Anna</u> kicked the ball out of bounds.

   _____ kicked the ball out of bounds.
   (She, Her)

4. The coach talked to <u>the players</u>.

   The coach talked to _____.
   (they, them)

If the team was an all-boys soccer team, would any of the pronouns used above change? Explain.

_____

_____

Lesson 1.4 Reflexive Pronouns

Reflexive pronouns are object pronouns that end in *-self* or *-selves* . They are used when the subject and object of a sentence are the same. Some reflexive pronouns are: *myself*, *yourself*, *himself*, *herself*, *itself*, *ourselves*, and *themselves*.

I can tie my shoes all by **myself**.   Do you talk to **yourself**?

> **Complete each sentence with a reflexive pronoun.**

1. Carlos finished the Super Sundae _____ .

2. I tied my sneakers all by _____ .

3. Jill and Charlie made _____ a snack.

4. Angie finished the project _____ .

5. Did that glass move _____ ?

6. My brother and I cleaned the kitchen _____ .

Can you write a sentence using the reflexive pronoun *yourself*? Try it!

_____

_____

Lesson 1.4 Reflexive Pronouns

In the situation below, Kyle's older sister is in charge of checking off the chore chart before school. Complete their conversation with reflexive pronouns.

Did you take out the garbage?

Did Manny make his bed?

Yes. I did it _____ .

Yes. He did it _____ .

Did you and Manny fold the laundry?

Did you make me breakfast?

Yes, we did it _____ .

Ugh. Make it _____ !

Lesson 1.5 Indefinite Pronouns

Indefinite pronouns do not refer to any particular person, place, or thing. They do not identify who or what is being referred to. Some indefinite pronouns are in the chart.

	any-	every-	no-	some-
People	anyone, anybody	everyone, everybody	no one, nobody	someone, somebody
Places	anywhere	everywhere	nowhere	somewhere
Things	anything	everything	nothing	something

Complete each sentence with an indefinite pronoun.

1. This weekend was boring. I did _____ .

2. I called the store, but _____ answered the phone.

3. Jamal left his notebook _____ , but he can't remember where.

4. Pippa had an upset stomach, so she didn't eat _____ for lunch.

5. With a flat tire, my dad's car was going _____ .

Lesson 1.5 Indefinite Pronouns

Complete each sentence with an indefinite pronoun from the box.

1. Why has _____ turned in their assignment?

2. I didn't want _____ to join me on my walk.

3. Henri cleaned _____ up off his bedroom floor.

4. Mrs. Bittle doesn't care where she goes for vacation, she just wants to go _____ .

5. Tarek couldn't think of _____ to get his friend for his birthday.

6. The volcano was shooting ash and lava

_____ .

no one
something
everything
nothing
everywhere
anybody
anywhere

Can you find and circle the indefinite pronoun that is left in the box? Try using it in a sentence.

_____

_____

Lesson 1.6 Verbs

Verbs tell what happens in a sentence. They are often action words.

Sadie **races** down the stairs. She **barks** at the cat on the windowsill.

> Read each sentence. Underline the verb. Write the letters of the verb on the lines.

1. Akiko places her new puppy on the rug in the living room.

2. The puppy sniffs the rug and the couch.

3. The puppy runs in circles around the room.

4. Akiko and her dad giggle at the excited little dog.

5. The puppy chews on Akiko's pink slipper.

> Write the circled letters from your answers to spell out the puppy's name. Start with a capital letter.

_____ _____ _____ _____ _____

Name _____

Lesson 1.6 Verbs

Complete each sentence with a verb from the box.

| run | take | give | throws | play | chase |

1. Sam and Hailey _____ their dogs to the park.

2. The dogs _____ in a pond.

3. They _____ around the park again and again.

4. Hailey _____ a stick.

5. The two dogs _____ the stick.

6. Sam and Hailey _____ lots of pets and kisses.

Can you illustrate one of the verbs from above? Try it!

Lesson 1.7 Adjectives

Adjectives are words that describe. They give more information about nouns. Adjectives often answer the questions *What kind?* or *How many?*

Kyle has a shirt. *What kind?* ⎯⎯⎯⎯⎯→ Kyle has a **striped** shirt.

Put flowers in that vase. *How many?* ⎯→ Put **ten** flowers in that vase.

> **Use an adjective from the box to describe each noun.**

green	rough	tiny	warm	noisy	furry

1. the _____ sunshine

2. a _____ bird

3. the _____ grass

4. a _____ squirrel

5. the _____ rock

6. a _____ lawnmower

 Can you write a sentence that uses two adjectives to describe a noun? Try it!

_____

_____

Name _____

Lesson 1.7 Adjectives

Read each sentence. Circle the adjective. Then, underline the noun the adjective describes.

Example: Kirsten made (sweet) lemonade.

1. A large raccoon lives near my house.

2. Raccoons have bushy tails.

3. Raccoons also have dark rings on their tails.

4. They have black patches on their faces.

5. They sleep in warm dens in the winter.

6. Raccoons eat fresh fruit, eggs, and insects.

 Can you write a sentence that describes an animal you have seen in the wild? Try it!

_____

_____

Lesson 1.8 Adverbs

Adverbs are words that can describe verbs. Adverbs often answer the questions *How? When?* or *Where?*

She opened the umbrella. *How?* ⟶ She **quickly** opened the umbrella.

We will go to the museum. *When?* ⟶ We will go **later** to the museum.

Matt fell. *Where?* ⟶ Matt fell **down**.

Circle the adverb in each sentence. Then, write *when*, *where*, or *how* to tell how the adverb describes the verb.

1. Yesterday, it snowed. _____

2. Big flakes fell gently to the ground. _____

3. Ian looked everywhere for his mittens. _____

4. He quickly put on his boots and hat. _____

5. He opened the door and walked outside. _____

6. Ian quietly listened to the falling snow. _____

Explain what part of speech in a sentence can help you find the adverb.

_____

_____

Name _____

Lesson 1.8 Adverbs

Some **adverbs** end with the letters *-ly*.

The leaf fell **slowly** from the tree.   Mom **softly** kissed my forehead.

> Complete each sentence with the correct adverb.

1. Ian _____ ran to his friend Ming's house.
   (quickly, quick)

2. He knocked _____ at the back door.
   (loud, loudly)

3. Ming _____ joined Ian in the yard.
   (happy, happily)

4. Ian _____ tossed a snowball at his friend.
   (playful, playfully)

5. Ming and Ian _____ drank hot cocoa.
   (gladly, glad)

Can you write a sentence about something you did with a friend? Try it! Use one adverb that ends in *-ly*.

_____

_____

Review Chapter 1

Circle the common nouns. Draw an **X** on the collective nouns. Underline the proper nouns.

1. Tasha and Sabrina's family lives on Glenwood Avenue.

2. Their neighbors, Nate and Bryan Cullen live in the house across the street.

3. Nate and Tasha take the bus to Bellevue Elementary School.

4. Mrs. Cullen took their litter of puppies to Miller Vet Hospital for shots.

Circle the pronouns and underline the reflexive pronouns in the sentences.

5. Bryan reminded himself to call Sabrina on Monday.

6. He needed to tell her about a club meeting.

7. It started at 4:00.

8. "We can walk there ourselves," he thought.

Review Chapter 1

Look at the underlined word in each sentence. Circle **adjective** or **adverb**.

9. <u>Yesterday</u>, Carlos and Grandpa walked to the pool.

   adjective   adverb

10. The <u>pool</u> water was cool to touch.

    adjective   adverb

11. Carlos and Grandpa <u>quickly</u> jumped in the pool.

    adjective   adverb

12. Grandpa swam <u>twenty</u> laps.

    adjective   adverb

Draw lines to complete the definitions.

13. An adjective   describes a noun.

14. A verb   can describe a verb.

15. A pronoun   tells what happens in a sentence.

16. An adverb   takes the place of a noun.

Chapter 2: Sentences •

Students will learn about sentences in Chapter 2. First, four different types of sentences are introduced—statements, commands, questions, and exclamations.

While statements and commands look quite similar, students will be asked to differentiate between the two. Does a sentence give information, or does it give a command? They both end with periods, so students will need to determine the intent of the sentence to figure out which type it is. Hint: statements usually begin with a noun or pronoun while commands usually begin with a verb.

Questions, with their question mark at the end, are easier to identify. Talk with students about the variety of questions that can be asked, such as *who*, *what, when, where, why*, and *how*. Exclamations are sentences that show excitement or surprise. Exclamations can even be one word sentences. They end with exclamation points.

Students are also shown that combining related sentences into one can make writing less choppy and more interesting for the reader. Students will learn how to combine sentences that share similar nouns, verbs, or adjectives. Learning to expand sentences with adjectives and adverbs is essential for students learning to make their writing more interesting for readers.

Skills Checklist •

☐ Identifying the different types of sentences including statements, commands, questions, and exclamations

☐ Learning to combine sentences that share similar nouns, verbs, or adjectives

☐ Learning to expand sentences by adding adjectives and adverbs to increase interest in their writing

Helpful Definitions ••

statement: something that is said in words; ends with a period; Examples: *I like pizza. It will rain all day.*

question: a sentence that asks for information; ends with a question mark; Examples: *What time is band practice? Did you pass your test?*

exclamation: a sentence that shows surprise, excitement, or other strong feeling; ends with an exclamation point; Examples: *That tastes gross! I am so happy for you!*

command: a sentence that gives an order or tells someone to do something; ends with a period; Examples: *Eat your dinner. Sit down.*

Tools and Tips •••

Play a game of charades to help your student understand the different types of sentences. Write several different sentence examples on index cards. Give your student a card to read and act out. Your student should use their body language and expressions to help clue the guesser in on what the sentence is. By acting out sentence types, your student will gain a better sense of what the different sentences convey to a reader.

To help your student learn to expand sentences for better writing, write on a strip of paper a simple sentence such as, *The dog ran.* Cut apart the sentence between each word. Discuss with your student the picture the sentence creates in one's mind. Ask them what they "see." Draw a picture to match the sentence to illustrate how detail is missing from the sentence. Have your student spread out the words of the original simple sentence and write additional words (adjectives and/or adverbs) to place before or after the noun and verb. Challenge your student to make the sentence a certain number of words long or to include a certain number of adjectives.

Lesson 2.1 Statements

A **statement** is a telling sentence. It begins with a capital letter and ends with a period.

My brother and I fly kites when we go to the beach.
My kite is shaped like a diamond.
It is purple, blue, and green.

Rewrite each statement. Begin with a capital letter and end with a period.

1. you do not need wind to fly a kite

    _____

2. some kites are shaped like dragons or fish

    _____

3. others are shaped like birds

    _____

4. flying kites is a fun hobby

    _____

Can you draw a kite you would like to fly? Try it! Then, write a statement about it.

_____

_____

_____

Name _____

Lesson 2.1 Statements

Example: N̲i̲c̲k and Matt made a kite shaped like a frog⦿

early kites were made in China. They were covered with silk Other

kites were covered with paper. the material covering the wooden sticks was

sometimes painted by hand

benjamin Franklin did experiments with kites Alexander Graham Bell also

used kites in his experiments.

today, kite festivals are held in many cities. people come from all around

the world They like to share their kites with

other kite lovers. some kites are tiny Others

are as much as one hundred feet long

Explain why using a period at the end of a statement is important.

_____

_____

Lesson 2.2 Questions

Questions are sentences that ask something. A question begins with a capital letter and ends with a question mark. Questions often begin with words such as *who, what, when, where, why, how, did, do, will,* and *can.*

Where are your shoes?   **When** did you see them?

Read the letter. Find and circle the incorrect ending punctuation marks. Write a question mark above each incorrect mark.

Dear Taylor,

How are you. I am having a great time on vacation. Have you ever been to Florida. I have never seen so many palm trees. Yesterday, we went to the ocean. Can you guess what I found on the beach. I found a jellyfish and sand dollar. We had a cookout with my cousins on Tuesday. I tried three kinds of fresh fish. Do you like fish. I like it more than I thought I would. That is all the news from Florida. I hope you are having a good vacation too.

Your friend,

Isabel

Can you write a question you would ask Isabel about her vacation? Try it!

_____

_____

Lesson 2.2 Questions

> Read each sentence. If the sentence is a statement, add a period. If a sentence is a question, add a question mark.

1. Isabel and her family drove to Florida

2. Do you know how long it took them to get there

3. They drove for three days

4. Isabel has two sisters

5. What did the girls do during the long drive

6. Did they play games in the car

7. Everyone in Isabel's family likes to surf

8. Where will they go on vacation next year

Lesson 2.3 Exclamations

Exclamations are sentences that are said with great feeling. They show excitement or surprise. Exclamations begin with a capital letter and end with an exclamation point. Some exclamations can be a single word.

Tanisha won the race!   Surprise!

> Rewrite each sentence. Each exclamation should begin with a capital letter and end with an exclamation point.

1. we won the game

   _____

2. maggie hit six home runs

   _____

3. she set a record

   _____

4. we are the champions

   _____

5. congratulations

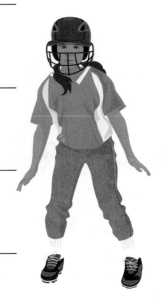

   _____

 Can you think of something exciting to tell a friend? Try it!

_____

_____

Name _____

Lesson 2.3 Exclamations

Read the diary entry. Find and circle the incorrect ending punctuation marks. Write an exclamation point above each incorrect mark.

Tuesday, April 7

Dear Diary,

Today began like any other day. I had no idea what was in store for me. I brought the mail in the house. There was a blue envelope. Hooray. It was just what I'd been waiting for. I opened it and pulled out the letter. Here is what it said: Congratulations. You are the grand-prize winner.

I ran upstairs to find my mom. I couldn't wait to tell her the news. We'd won a free vacation. I knew she'd be amazed. I enter many contests. I don't usually win, though. What a great day!

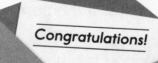

Congratulations!

Explain what an exclamation point tells a reader.

_____

_____

_____

Lesson 2.4 Commands

Commands are sentences that tell you to do something. Commands begin with a capital letter. They end with a period. Commands often begin with a verb.

Put away your coat and bag.   Close the door.

> Read each sentence. If it is a command, write **C** on the line. If it is a statement, write **S** on the line.

1. Tia and her grandpa like to make empanadas. _____

2. They follow special rules in the kitchen. _____

3. Wash your hands before you cook or bake. _____

4. Be careful around a hot stove. _____

5. Read the recipe before you begin. _____

6. Measure the ingredients. _____

7. Tia makes the empanada dough. _____

8. Grandpa teaches Tia how to roll the dough. _____

Name _____

Lesson 2.4 Commands

Choose a verb from the box to begin each command. Then, add the correct
end mark.

| Drink | Fill | Chop | Blend | Put | Turn |

How to Make a "Berry" Good Smoothie

1. _____ a banana into small pieces

2. _____ some berries and the banana pieces in the blender

3. _____ the blender halfway with milk and orange juice

4. _____ on the blender

5. _____ the ingredients until they are smooth

6. _____ the smoothie from a tall glass

 Can you think of a rule you have to follow at home? Write it as
a command.

_____

_____

Name _____

Lesson 2.5 Combining Sentences (Nouns)

Sometimes, sentences can be **combined** to make writing easier and more enjoyable to read. The two sentences can be combined by using the word *and* between the **nouns** in the new sentence.

<u>Bats</u> eat flies. <u>Frogs</u> eat flies.

(*Both sentences tell about things that eat flies, so they can be combined.*)

<u>Bats</u> **and** <u>frogs</u> eat flies.

> Read each pair of sentences. If the sentences can be joined with the word *and*, make a √ on the line. If not, make an **X** on the line.

1. Blue jays visit my birdfeeder. Robins visit my birdfeeder. _____

2. Parrots live in warm places. Penguins live in cold places. _____

3. Hawks build nests on ledges. Eagles build nests on ledges. _____

4. Hummingbirds like flowers. Bees like flowers. _____

5. Geese fly south for the winter. Owls do not fly south in the winter. _____

Can you think of a way to combine one of the sentence pairs you marked with an X so that they can be combined? Try it!

_____

_____

Name _____

Lesson 2.5 Combining Sentences (Nouns)

Combine each pair of sentences into one sentence. Write the new sentence.

1. Herons live near water. Mallards live near water.

_____

2. Sparrows are mostly brown. Wrens are mostly brown.

_____

3. Cardinals eat seeds. Finches eat seeds.

_____

_____

4. Crows have black feathers. Grackles have black feathers.

_____

_____

Explain when a writer can combine sentences and when a writer cannot combine sentences.

_____

_____

_____

Lesson 2.6 Combining Sentences (Verbs)

Sometimes, sentences can be **combined** to make text flow better. The two sentences can be combined into one by using the word **and** between the **verbs** in the new sentence.

Julia <u>bikes</u> on Saturdays. Julia <u>jogs</u> on Saturdays.

(Both sentences tell what Julia does on Saturdays, so they can be combined.)

Julia <u>bikes</u> **and** <u>jogs</u> on Saturdays.

> Read the sentences. Complete each combined sentence with the missing word or words.

1. Mom carried out the birthday cake. Mom placed it on the table.

    _____ carried out the birthday cake _____ placed it on the table.

2. Carmen took a deep breath. Carmen blew out the candles.

    _____ took a deep breath _____ blew out the candles.

3. The children sang "Happy Birthday." The children clapped for Carmen.

    _____ sang "Happy Birthday" _____ clapped for Carmen.

 Can you write a combined sentence that tells two things you did at a party? Try it!

_____

_____

Lesson 2.6 Combining Sentences (Verbs)

Combine each pair of sentences into one sentence.

1. Carmen unwrapped her presents. Carmen opened the boxes.

   _____

   _____

2. Carmen smiled. Carmen thanked her friends for the gifts.

   _____

   _____

3. Everyone played freeze tag. Everyone had a good time.

   _____

   _____

4. The guests ate cake. The guests drank pink lemonade.

   _____

   _____

Lesson 2.7 Combining Sentences (Adjectives)

Sometimes, sentences can be **combined** to make text more enjoyable to read. The two sentences can be combined into one by using the word **and** between the **adjectives** in the new sentence.

The wagon is <u>red</u>. The wagon is <u>shiny</u>.

(The adjectives *red* and *shiny* both describe *wagon*).

The wagon is <u>red</u> **and** <u>shiny</u>.

> Read each pair of sentences. If the adjectives in both sentences describe the same person or thing, the sentences can be combined. If the two sentences can be combined write a ✓ on the line. If they cannot be combined, write an **X**.

1. The paints are shiny. The paints are wet. _____

2. The afternoon is warm. The evening is sunny. _____

3. Oliver has a new paintbrush. Dad has a new canvas. _____

4. The wall is large. The wall is white. _____

5. The tulips are red. The windmill is tall. _____

Can you change one of the sentence pairs that have an *X* so that they can be combined? Try it!

_____

_____

Name _____

Lesson 2.7 Combining Sentences (Adjectives)

Combine each pair of sentences into one sentence. You may not have to use the word *and*.

Example: Oliver opened his new paints. His paints are watercolor paints.

Oliver opened his new watercolor paints.

1. Oliver's painting is bright. Oliver's painting is cheerful.

   _____

2. Oliver painted a flower garden. The garden was colorful.

   _____

3. Oliver's art is beautiful. Oliver's art is popular.

   _____

4. The red tulips are his favorite. The tulips are pretty.

   _____

 Explain why a writer might combine two sentences that describe the same thing.

_____

_____

Lesson 2.8 Expanding Sentences

Expanding sentences adds detail to simple sentences. By adding **adjectives** and **adverbs**, a writer makes sentences more interesting to a reader. The expanded sentence can also provide more information.

The car raced. ⎯⎯⎯⎯⎯⎯⎯→ The **fast red** car raced **over the line.**

Expand each simple sentence.

1. A dog barked.

    _____

2. The teacher spoke.

    _____

3. The girl laughed.

    _____

4. A snake hissed.

    _____

Can you make one of your sentences even longer? Try it!

_____

_____

Lesson 2.8 Expanding Sentences

Sometimes you can add **transitional words** or **prepositional phrases** to simple sentences. These words and phrases add more detail by telling *when*, *where*, and *how*.

Gus was sick. ⟶ **Last week, my friend** Gus was sick **with a nasty cold.**

> Read each pair of sentences. Underline the words in the second sentence that add more detail to the first sentence.

1. My father drove.

Yesterday, my father drove us to the beach to play in the ocean.

2. We threw a frisbee.

When we arrived, we threw a frisbee to my rescue dog named Patches.

3. I flew my kite.

Before we left, I flew my kite high in the air.

Can you expand one of the above simple sentences in a different way? Try it!

_____

Review Chapter 2

Decide if each sentence is a statement (**S**), question (**Q**), exclamation (**E**), or command (**C**). Circle the letter. Then, rewrite each sentence using correct capitalization and ending punctuation.

1. take the trash to the curb   S   Q   E   C

_____

2. what time do you need to wake up   S   Q   E   C

_____

3. nat got a new wheel for her hamster   S   Q   E   C

_____

4. that saxophone player is amazing   S   Q   E   C

_____

5. can we have pasta for dinner tonight   S   Q   E   C

_____

6. this was the best day ever   S   Q   E   C

_____

7. get the ladder from the garage   S   Q   E   C

_____

8. matt drives a large white truck   S   Q   E   C

_____

Review Chapter 2

Combine each pair of sentences. Write the new sentence.

9. Maria likes chocolate ice cream. Mateo likes chocolate ice cream.

_____

10. Izzy jumped into the lake. Izzy got the ball.

_____

11. Lee's shoes are red. Lee's shoes are new.

_____

12. Our backyard has yellow tulips. Our backyard has red tulips.

_____

13. Kickball is fun in PE class. Yoga is fun in PE class.

_____

14. The storm was loud. The storm was scary.

_____

Expand each simple sentence.

15. The owl screeched.

_____

16. My friend cried.

_____

Chapter 3: Capitalization

Chapter 3 is all about capitalization! Whether students are writing a story or report, starting a journal entry with a date, or texting a friend about their new favorite movie, they need to know which words should begin with a capital letter. There are so many reasons to capitalize letters, and this chapter is a great place to start for second graders.

Capital letters call out important points or information in writing. A capital letter can signal that a new sentence is beginning. It can alert a reader that what they're reading is someone's name or title, such as Dr. Wilhelm, or that they're reading about a specific place, like Cedar Rapids, Iowa. Students will also learn about and practice capitalizing dates, holidays, and titles of books, movies, and songs.

Skills Checklist

☐ Learning to capitalize the first word in a sentence

☐ Learning to capitalize names of specific people and places

☐ Learning to capitalize titles of respect

☐ Learning to capitalize days, months, and holidays

☐ Learning to capitalize titles of books, movies, and other works

Helpful Definitions

capital: an uppercase letter of the alphabet; Examples: *A, Z*

proper noun: a word that names a specific person, place, thing, or idea; begins with a capital letter; Examples: *Nintendo, Mount Everest, Jonas*

title (1): a word or group of words attached to a person's name to show respect, honor, or rank; Examples: *Sir, Mister, Doctor*

title (2): the name given to something, such as a book or song, to identify it; Examples: <u>*Stuart Little*</u>, "*Happy Birthday*"

Tools and Tips

A word association may help your student learn when to capitalize a person's name and title. The word *capital* looks like the word *captain*. The captain of a ship or airplane is very important. They deserve honor and respect so we capitalize their names and titles.

If your student is uncertain about when to use capital letters, remind them that a capital letter signals the start of a new sentence. Without that, a reader would be confused. As writers, we want our readers to be able to read our writing smoothly and find it easy to understand.

Special and specific names of people, places, and things will take time to understand. Cut out magazine clippings and advertisements to collect a sampling of special names that require capital letters.

Involve your student in creating a weekly or monthly calendar. Writing the days of the week, months of the year, and special days such as holidays, will give your student practice capitalizing these special words.

Lesson 3.1 Capitalizing the First Word in a Sentence

All sentences begin with a **capital letter**. A capital letter signals to the reader that a new sentence is starting.

> **M**arisol colored the leaves green.
> **I**s the book on the coffee table?
> **R**aise your left hand.

> Read and proofread the passage. To show that a letter should be a capital, underline it three times. Then, write the capital letter above it. The first one has been done for you.

T
tree trunks can tell the story of a tree's life. a

slice of a tree trunk shows many rings. a tree adds a

new ring every year. each ring has a light part and a

dark part.

when scientists look at the rings, they learn about the tree. the rings can tell

how old a tree is. they can tell what the weather was like. if there was a fire or a

flood, the rings will show it. trees cannot talk, but they do tell stories.

Lesson 3.1 Capitalizing the First Word in a Sentence

Rewrite each sentence below. Be sure your sentences begin with a capital letter.

1. the oldest living tree is in California.

_____

2. it is located in the White Mountains.

_____

3. the tree is more than 4,600 years old.

_____

4. scientists named the tree Methuselah.

_____

5. would you like to visit this tree one day?

_____

_____

Explain why starting a sentence with a capital letter is helpful to a reader.

_____

_____

Name _____

Lesson 3.2 Capitalizing Names

The name of a person, pet, or product always begins with a capital letter.

Jasper is Emily's brother.
The bear cub's name is Arthur.
I always use Sniffy's tissues.

Complete each sentence with the name in parentheses ( ). Remember to capitalize the names of people, pets, and products.

1. _____ (cassie's) favorite food is cookies.

2. My parakeet, _____ (prudence), eats

   _____ (pet food plus) peanuts.

3. _____ (apple o's) is

   _____ (amy's) favorite cereal.

4. _____ (bradley's) bunny, _____ (boris), eats beets.

5. _____ (tess) and _____ (tom) like

   _____ (tito's tasty tacos).

 Can you find the name of a product nearby? Write its name.

_____

Spectrum Language Arts **Grade 2**

Lesson 3.2 Capitalizing Names

> Read the paragraph. To show that a letter should be a capital, underline it three times. Then, write the capital letter above it. The first one has been done for you.

The neighborhood was getting ready to have a pet show. G̲ geoffrey and gina

brushed their pet gerbil, george, with a groom-easy brush they bought at the

pet store. hank and harry's hamster, hilda, was ready to perform all her tricks.

Sandeep tightly held his snake, simon.

The show was ready to start. Only dominique and her dog, dora, were still

missing. dominique had to finish giving dora a

bath with clean critters shampoo. Finally, they

arrived. The pet show could begin!

Imagine that you are asked to name a new pet food. What would you call it? Write the product name.

_____

Lesson 3.3 Capitalizing Titles

A **title** is a word that comes before a person's name. A title gives more information about who a person is. Titles that come before a name begin with a capital letter.

Grandma Jean   Uncle Davis   Cousin Ella
President Adams   Doctor Wright   Judge Thomas

Titles of respect also begin with a capital letter.

Miss Sullivan   Mrs. Chun   Mr. Garza

> Read and proofread the diary entry. To show that a letter should be a capital, underline it three times. Then, write the capital letter above it. The first one has been done for you.

Dear Diary,

    Last night, I went to a play with <u>a</u>unt Sonia and uncle Pat. I sat next to

cousin Fiona and cousin Nora. The play was about ms. Amelia Earhart, the first

woman to fly across the Atlantic Ocean alone. ms. Earhart led an exciting life.

She even met president Roosevelt.

    After the play, I met Aunt Sonia's friend, mrs. Angley. She played the role

of ms. Earhart. I also met mr. Roche. He played the role of president Roosevelt.

He was very kind and funny.

Lesson 3.3 Capitalizing Titles

Rewrite each of the following sentences. Remember, titles begin with a capital letter.

1. ms. Earhart lived an exciting life.

_____

2. mr. Putnam published a book about her.

_____

3. grandpa Leo gave aunt Sonia the book.

_____

4. she just read a book about mrs. Roosevelt.

_____

Can you think of a person from history you would like to meet? Write their name and include their title.

_____

Lesson 3.4 Capitalizing Place Names

The names of special **places** always begin with a capital letter.

Garner Science Museum   Donovan Street   France

Orlando, Florida   Mississippi River   Mars

> Complete each sentence with the word in parentheses ( ). Remember, special places begin with a capital letter.

1. My family left Sonoma, _____ , yesterday morning.
   (california)

2. We waved good-bye to our house on _____ .
   (clancy avenue)

3. We passed _____ .
   (washington elementary school)

4. We crossed the _____ .
   (golden gate bridge)

5. We were on our way across the _____ !
   (united states)

Name _____

Lesson 3.4 Capitalizing Place Names

Read and proofread the postcard. Underline each letter that should be a capital three times. Then, write the capital letter above it. The first one has been done for you.

Hi annie,

   I am writing from arizona. Today, we went

to the tucson children's museum. Tomorrow, we

will head to the grand canyon. Next week, we'll

be in california. We will visit stanford university.

That is where my parents went to college. Then,

we will head north. I can't wait to see redwood

national forest.

USA

Annie Schneider

452 cherry lane

charlotte, NC 22471

                                    Your pal,

                                    Priya

Can you think of a city and state you would like to visit? Write it.

_____

Lesson 3.5 Capitalizing Days, Months, and Holidays

The days of the week each begin with a capital letter.

Sunday, Monday, Tuesday, Wednesday, Thursday, Friday, Saturday

The months of the year are also capitalized.

January, February, March, April, May, June, July,
August, September, October, November, December

The names of holidays begin with a capital letter.

Valentine's Day   Memorial Day   Thanksgiving

Read the sentences. Circle each word that should start with a capital letter.

1. I have to go to the doctor on monday.

2. Softball practice starts on tuesday afternoon.

3. new year's day is january 1.

4. There is no school on presidents' day.

5. I will go to my piano lesson on friday.

6. We will go to the grocery store on saturday morning.

JANUARY						
S	M	T	W	TH	F	S
	1 ★	2	3	4	5	6
7	8 Doctor	9	10	11	12	13
14	15	16	17	18	19 Piano Lessons	20
21	22	23	24	25	26	27
28	29	30	31			

Lesson 3.5 Capitalizing Days, Months, and Holidays

The Johnson family keeps a list of important holidays and dates. Rewrite each special day correctly.

Ella's birthday january 20 _____

valentine's Day February 14 _____

Shane's party may 11 _____

Kahlil's first birthday june 22 _____

the Cheswicks' trip july 18 _____

thanksgiving November 23 _____

Tyson's birthday december 29 _____

Can you write a sentence about something that happened this week or month? Try it!

_____

_____

Name _____

Review Chapter 3

Rewrite the following sentences with capital letters where they are needed.

1. president kennedy liked animals.

    _____

2. charlie and pushinka were two of his dogs.

    _____

3. his daughter, caroline, had a pony named macaroni.

    _____

4. mrs. jackie kennedy had a horse named sardar.

    _____

Read the paragraph. Write the words that should be capitalized on the lines.

President coolidge had many pets. some pets were ordinary pets. For example, he had a dog named blackberry and a canary named snowflake. others were more unusual. he also had a raccoon named horace. president Coolidge even had a donkey named ebenezer. mrs. Coolidge must have liked animals too!

5. _____ 6. _____ 7. _____

8. _____ 9. _____ 10. _____

11. _____ 12. _____ 13. _____ 14. _____

Review Chapter 3

> Complete each sentence with the word or words in parentheses ( ). Capitalize the names of special places.

15. Take _____ (maple street) to the end.

16. You will pass _____ (wintergreen school).

17. Turn left on _____ (westbury avenue).

18. In about a mile, you will see _____ (lane pool).

19. Turn right on _____ (pine hill drive).

20. Cross _____ (stony creek), and continue for two miles.

21. You will see a _____ (michigan) flag by the front door of our house.

> Read each sentence. If the sentence is correct, make a ✓ on the line. If it is incorrect, make an **X** on the line and circle the letter or letters that should be capitalized.

22. _____ In December, Uncle Jack flew to Paris.

23. _____ He said he would like to live in france one day.

24. _____ Then, he took a train to Switzerland for christmas.

25. _____ He went skiing in the Swiss Alps.

26. _____ Uncle Jack called to say happy birthday to me on saturday, march 4.

27. _____ One day, he will take me to paris, rome, and berlin.

Chapter 4: Punctuation

Just like the beginning of a sentence gets special treatment with a capital letter, the end of a sentence gets special treatment with a punctuation mark. But many punctuation marks can be found elsewhere, too, and Chapter 4 covers different types of punctuation marks and where they should go.

In this chapter, students will have practice choosing the correct ending punctuation based on whether a sentence is stating information, showing emotion, or asking a question. Students will also practice using periods in words that are abbreviated, such as *Mr.*, *Aug.*, and *St.*

Not only are commas used in dates, such as *May 15, 2023*, but also with cities and states, like *Houston, Texas*. Commas are also used to separate items in a series, or list, so they don't run together, and to join two sentences together with a conjunction.

Chapter 4 will give students practice with where to place quotation marks and ending punctuation in dialogue.

Finally, students will learn how to correctly punctuate titles of works, like songs, poems, books, and more.

Skills Checklist

- [ ] Using ending punctuation at the ends of statements, commands, questions, and exclamations

- [ ] Using periods in abbreviations

- [ ] Using commas with dates, cities, and states; in a series of items; in dialogue; letters; and in compound sentences

- [ ] Using quotation marks in dialogue

- [ ] Using apostrophes in possessives

- [ ] Punctuating titles of books and other works

period: the punctuation mark (.) used to show that a sentence has ended or that a word has been abbreviated; Examples: I will be home later. Dr. Winston set my broken bone.

question mark: the punctuation mark (?) that follows a question; Examples: Did you hear that? Is your dad coming to pick us up?

exclamation point: the punctuation mark (!) used at the end of a sentence that shows surprise, excitement, or other strong feeling; Examples: Wow, you did great! Watch out for the tree!

comma: the punctuation mark (,) used for separating parts of a sentence, words in a list, or groups of three digits in large numbers; Examples: Once I got to the park, I ran to the tire swing. My favorite colors are red, green, and orange.

apostrophe: a punctuation mark (') that is used with the letter *s* to show ownership or to show where letters have been left off; Examples: Serena's shoes, my teacher's desk, haven't, we've

quotation marks: punctuation marks (" ") used to show where speech begins and ends; Examples: "Is everyone alright?" asked the police officer. Tomas said, "I knew I was late."

Tools and Tips ••

Ask your student to demonstrate their new knowledge of punctuation by creating a poster. The poster could be an advertisement or an informational poster about a famous person. Enourage your student to use every type of punctuation learned in this chapter. For example, if a famous person is the chosen topic, research some of their famous quotations to practice using quotation marks and commas. If an advertisement is chosen, be sure your student understands which parts of the text need punctuation marks to entice a customer to read the advertisement.

Name _____

Lesson 4.1 Periods

Periods are used at the ends of statements and commands. They tell the reader that a sentence has ended.

    We ate tomato soup for lunch.
    It will probably rain this afternoon.

Read and proofread the paragraph. Add periods where they are needed.

Example: I see a brown bug.

Most people do not like mosquitoes If you spend any time outside in

the summer, you will probably get bitten Not all mosquitoes bite people Only

female mosquitoes bite people When mosquitoes

bite, they take a drop of blood from a person Some

mosquitoes like birds or flowers better

Explain why using a period in your writing is important.

_____

_____

Lesson 4.1 Periods

Read the sentences. Add a period to the end of each statement.

1. There are thousands of types of mosquitoes

2. Mosquitoes like human sweat

3. Some people never get mosquito bites

4. Mosquitoes lay eggs in still water

5. Bug spray can protect you from bites

Imagine you are about to hike a rainforest trail that has many mosquitoes. There is a sign at the beginning telling you what to do to protect yourself. Draw the sign. Include at least five commands you might read on the sign.

Lesson 4.2 Question Marks

A question ends with a **question mark**.

Where did you put the crayons?   What time will Grandpa get here?

> Read each answer (**A**). Then, write the question (**Q**) that was asked to get that answer. The first one has been done for you.

1.   Q: <u>What did you eat for dinner?</u>

   A: I ate spaghetti for dinner.

2.   Q: _____

   A: My skateboard is in the garage.

3.   Q: _____

   A: Keiko went to the library.

4.   Q: _____

   A: Ashton is seven years old.

5.   Q: _____

   A: Mr. Arnold lives in Houston.

6.   Q: _____

   A: The book is about a boy who wishes he could fly.

Name _____

Lesson 4.2 Question Marks

Theo is asking an author questions for a school report. Cross out the incorrectly used end marks. Write the correct end marks. The first one has been done for you.

Theo: What do you like about being a writer

Ms. Li: I love to tell stories.

Theo: Where do you get your ideas.

Ms. Li: I used to be a teacher? Many ideas come from my students.

Theo: When do you write.

Ms. Li: I write for about four hours every morning?

Theo: Do you have any hobbies.

Ms. Li: I like to garden, ski, and do crossword puzzles.

Can you write a question you would like to ask the author of your favorite book? Try it!

_____

_____

Lesson 4.3 Exclamation Points

An **exclamation point** is used to end a sentence that is exciting. Sometimes exclamation points are used to show surprise.

Look at the rainbow!   I loved that movie!   Wow!

Read the poster. Add the missing end marks where they are needed.

Hooray

The Bellview Fair

is coming to town in July

Win great prizes

Ride the biggest Ferris wheel in Clark County

Admission is $3.00 for adults and $2.00 for kids under twelve

Sample tasty foods

The fair opens July 6 and closes July 12

Don't miss all the fun

Lesson 4.3 Exclamation Points

Read each pair of sentences. One sentence should end with a period. The other should end with an exclamation point. Add the correct end marks.

1. I went to the Bellview Fair

   I had the best time

2. I played a game called Toss the Ring

   I won four stuffed animals

3. All the sheep escaped from their pen

   It did not take the farmers long to catch them, though

4. I ate a snow cone and some cotton candy

   The cotton candy got stuck in my hair

Can you write an exclamation about an exciting place you've been? Try it!

_____

_____

Lesson 4.4 Periods in Abbreviations

An **abbreviation** is a short way of writing something. Most abbreviations are followed by a **period**.

The days of the week can be abbreviated.
Sun.   Mon.   Tues.   Wed.   Thurs.   Fri.   Sat.

Most months of the year can be abbreviated. (*May*, *June*, and *July* are not abbreviated because their names are so short.)
Jan.   Feb.   Mar.   Apr.   Aug.   Sept.   Oct.   Nov.   Dec.

People's titles are almost always abbreviated when they come before a name.
Missus = **Mrs.**   Mister = **Mr.**   Doctor = **Dr.**

Types of streets are abbreviated in addresses.
Street = **St.**   Avenue = **Ave.**   Drive = **Dr.** Lane = **Ln.**

> Look at each underlined word. Write the letter of the correct abbreviation on the line.

1. _____ 19052 Inglewood <u>Avenue</u>   **a.**   Thurs.

2. _____ <u>Doctor</u> Weinstein   **b.**   Jan.

3. _____ <u>Thursday</u> night   **c.**   Dr.

4. _____ <u>October</u> 15, 2006   **d.**   Ln.

5. _____ 18 Winding Creek <u>Lane</u>   **e.**   Ave.

6. _____ <u>January</u> 1, 2000   **f.**   Oct.

Name _____

Lesson 4.4 Periods in Abbreviations

Write the abbreviation for each word in parentheses ( ).

Example: Sunday, _____ Nov. _____ 12
(November)

1. 4250 Rosehill _____
(Street)

2. _____ Ortega
(Mister)

3. _____ 4, 2014
(April)

4. _____ 10, 1904
(February)

5. _____ morning
(Wednesday)

6. _____ Pappas
(Missus)

7. Beech _____
(Drive)

Explain when a writer might use abbreviations.

_____

_____

Name _____

Lesson 4.5 Commas with Dates, Cities, and States

Commas are used in dates. They are used between the day of the month and the year.

   January 11, 1988   October 8, 1845   June 25, 2023
              ↑   ↑   ↑

Commas are also used between the names of cities and states. When the names of cities and states are in the middle of a sentence, a comma goes after the name of the state too.

   After we left Council Bluffs, Iowa, we headed north.
                           ↑   ↑

Read and proofread each sentence. Add the missing commas. The first one has been done for you.

1. Selma was born on August 16͵2008.

August						
S	M	T	W	TH	F	S
	1	2	3	4	5	6
7	8	9	10	11	12	13
14	15	16	17	18	19	20
21	22	23	24	25	26	27
28	29	30	31			

2. She lives in Taos New Mexico.

3. Her little sister was born on April 4 2012.

4. Selma's grandparents live in Denver Colorado.

5. It is a long drive from Denver Colorado to Taos New Mexico.

6. The last time Selma's grandparents visited was December 20 2013.

Lesson 4.5 Commas with Dates, Cities, and States

Read each sentence. If it is correct, write a ✓ on the line. If it is wrong, rewrite it.

1. Great Grandma was born on March, 4 1952. _____

   _____

2. Hef's family moved to Butte Montana when she was two. _____

   _____

3. My date of birth is May 27 2001. _____

   _____

4. The plane stopped in Baltimore, Maryland, to get more fuel. _____

   _____

5. It snowed eight inches in Stowe Vermont. _____

   _____

6. Cousin Sarah graduated on June 4, 2023. _____

   _____

7. Gum Spring, Virginia is where my grandma lives. _____

   _____

Lesson 4.6 Commas in Series

A **series** is a list of words. Use a **comma** after each word in the series except the last word.

The chef put carrots, tomatoes, and peppers in the pan.
                 ↑   ↑

Rewrite the sentences. Add the missing commas.

1. Mom got out a picnic basket plates and cups.

    _____

2. Lily packed forks knives spoons and napkins.

    _____

3. Amelia added pears oranges and apples.

    _____

4. Dad made sandwiches a salad and brownies.

    _____

Name _____

Lesson 4.6 Commas in Series

> Add commas where they are needed in each sentence.

Example: The dog had black, brown, and white spots in its fur.

1. Maranda Isabel and Carolyn came to my house for a sleepover.

2. Mr. Garcia caught Ricardo Jamie and Keira running through the halls.

3. "Should we go to the beach pool or park this afternoon?" asked Mrs. Sanchez.

4. In gym class we play basketball tennis and kickball.

5. When I am older I want to be either an astronaut a chef or a teacher.

6. For dinner my dad made us steak mashed potatoes and green beans.

Name _____

Lesson 4.7 Commas in Letters

In a letter, a **comma** follows the greeting and the closing.

Dear Mr. Wong,   Your friend,   Sincerely,
       ↑   ↑   ↑

> Circle the commas in the letter.

August 3, 2023

Dear Helga,

    It is hot and sunny here today. I am going to the park nearby to play in the splash pad with a few friends. Do you like to play in water?

    What is the weather like in Iceland this time of year? Please write back!

Your pen pal,

Amelia

Can you write the greeting and closing for a letter you would write to a friend? Try it!

_____

_____

Lesson 4.7 Commas in Letters

Read the letter. Add the missing commas where they are needed. The first one has been done for you.

June 19, 2022

Dear Grandma

    Yesterday, we went to the park. Lily Amelia and Mom shook out the picnic blanket. Dad carried the basket the drinks and the toys from the car. We all ate some salad a sandwich and a fruit.

    Deepak Sita and Raj were at the park with their parents too. We played tag and fed the ducks. Later, we shared our brownies with the Nair family. I wish you could have been there!

Love

Max

Lesson 4.8 Commas in Compound Sentences

A **compound sentence** is made up of two smaller sentences. The smaller sentences are joined by a comma and often the word *and* or *but* .

Michelle went to the store. She bought some markers.
Michelle went to the store, **and** she bought some markers.

Bats sleep during the day. They are active at night.
Bats sleep during the day, **but** they are active at night.

> Combine each pair of sentences by using a comma and the word *and* or *but*.

1. Abby rode her bike. Gilbert rode his scooter.

   _____

   _____

2. My new bedroom is big. My old bedroom was bigger.

   _____

   _____

3. The black cat is beautiful. The orange cat is friendly.

   _____

   _____

4. Roberto is a fast swimmer. Sophie is a faster swimmer.

   _____

   _____

Name _____

Lesson 4.8 Commas in Compound Sentences

Read and proofread the paragraph. Add commas where they are needed.

Example: My sleeves are short, but my pants are even shorter.

The leaves of the poison ivy plant are shaped like almonds and they come in

groups of three. Poison ivy can cause a rash and it can make you itch. The leaves

of the plant contain oil that causes the rash. Some people can touch the plant

but they will not get a rash. The oil can stick to your clothes. Washing with

soap and water removes the oil and it can keep the rash

from spreading.

Explain how looking for commas can help you find compound
sentences.

_____

_____

_____

Lesson 4.9 Apostrophes in Possessives

An **apostrophe** is a punctuation mark that can be used in a **possessive** noun. A possessive noun shows ownership. Use an apostrophe and the letter *s* at the end of a word to show that the person or thing is the owner.

the car's engine   Stacy's eyes

Jake's laugh   the table's leg

Rewrite each phrase as a possessive.

1. the lens of the camera

   _____

2. the spots of the leopard

   _____

3. the trip of Amy

   _____

4. the roar of the lion

   _____

5. the hat of Tim

   _____

6. the roof of the car

   _____

Name _____

Lesson 4.9 Apostrophes in Possessives

Read each phrase. Write the letter of the correctly written possessive on the line.

1. _____ the horn of the rhino

   a. the rhino's horn   **b.** the horn's rhino

2. _____ the animals of Africa

   a. the animal's of Africa   **b.** Africa's animals

3. _____ the photos of John

   a. John photo's   **b.** John's photos

4. _____ the favorite animal of Don

   a. Don's favorite animal's   **b.** Don's favorite animal

5. _____ the baby of the hippo

   a. the baby's hippo   **b.** the hippo's baby

6. _____ the tent of Sarah

   a. Sarah's tent   **b.** Sarah tent

 Can you write about a feature on a favorite animal? Try it! Use a possessive.

_____

_____

Lesson 4.10 Quotation Marks in Dialogue

Quotation marks are used around the exact words a person says. One set of quotation marks is used before the first word the person says. Another set is used at the end of the person's words. The exact words people say are sometimes called **dialogue**. Quotation marks are used to show which words are dialogue.

Jamal said, "I am going to play in a piano recital on Saturday."

"Do you like fresh apple pie?" asked the baker.

"Hooray!" shouted Sydney. "Today is a snow day!"

Remember to put the second pair of quotation marks after the punctuation mark that ends the sentence.

Read each sentence. Underline the speaker's exact words. Then, add a set of quotation marks before and after the speaker's words.

1. Would you like to go skiing this afternoon? asked Mom.

2. Alyssa asked, Where will we go?

3. Mom said, Wintergreen Mountain is not too far away.

4. Can I bring a friend? asked Zane.

5. Mom said, You can each bring along one friend.

6. Alyssa said, Riley will be so excited!

Spectrum Language Arts **Grade 2**

Lesson 4.10 Quotation Marks in Dialogue

> Read each sentence. Write the sentence again. Add quotation marks where they are needed. Remember to find the speaker's exact words first.

1. Have you ever been skiing? Zane asked his friend.

_____

_____

2. Joey said, No, but it sounds like fun.

_____

_____

3. Riley said, My grandpa taught me how to ski.

_____

_____

4. She added, He lives near the mountains in Vermont.

_____

_____

Lesson 4.11 Titles of Books and Movies

The titles of books and movies are underlined in text. This lets the reader know that the underlined words are part of a title.

> Cristina's favorite movie is <u>Because of Winn-Dixie</u>.
> Harry wrote a book report on <u>Nate the Great and the Musical Note</u>.

Underline the title of each book or movie.

1. Tom Hanks was the voice of Woody in the movie Toy Story.

2. Mara Wilson played Matilda Wormwood in the movie Matilda.

3. In the movie Shrek, Cameron Diaz was the voice of Princess Fiona.

4. The movie Fly Away Home is based on a true story.

5. Harriet the Spy is the name of a book and a movie.

Lesson 4.11 Titles of Books and Movies

Read the passage. Underline the titles.

Jon Scieszka (say *shess-ka*) is a popular author. He has written many books

for children. He is best known for his book The Stinky Cheese Man and Other

Fairly Stupid Tales. Jon has always loved books. Dr. Seuss's famous book Green

Eggs and Ham made Jon feel like he could be a writer one day. In 1989, Jon

wrote The True Story of the Three Little Pigs. Many

children think his books are very funny. They also like

the pictures. Lane Smith draws the pictures for many of Jon's books. They worked

together on the book Math Curse. Their book Science Verse is also popular.

Can you write the title of your favorite book? Try it!

_____

Review Chapter 4

Read each sentence. Add the correct end mark on the line.

1. Thursday started out like any other day_____

2. I ate breakfast and went to school_____

3. When I came home, my mom and dad told me the news_____

4. Do you know what they said_____

5. I am going to be a big brother_____

Rewrite each phrase. Use an abbreviation in place of the underlined word.

6. <u>Missus</u> Lahiri _____

7. Delmar <u>Lane</u> _____

8. Tuesday, <u>August</u> 2 _____

9. <u>November</u> 22, 2004 _____

10. <u>Doctor</u> White _____

Rewrite each phrase as a possessive.

11. the cat of Enrique _____

12. the shirt of Cassie _____

Review Chapter 4

Read the letter. Add the missing commas.

Dear Quinn

    I need to write a letter for school. I chose to write to you about Peter Jenkins. He was born on July 8 1951 in Greenwich Connecticut. Peter is best known for walking across America. He began his walk on October 15 1973. He walked from Alfred New York to Florence Oregon. His walk ended on January 18 1979.

    Today, Peter lives on a farm in Spring Hill Tennessee. His children are named Rebekah Jedidiah Luke Aaron Brooke and Julianne. Peter likes to travel write and speak to people about his adventures. I hope you liked learning about Peter. I'll talk to you soon!

Your friend
Eli

Complete each sentence with your own answer. Use quotation marks to show that someone is speaking. Don't forget to underline titles.

13. _____ is the funniest book I have ever read.

14. I think everyone should see the movie _____.

15. When she came from the dentist, Beatriz said, _____.

16. Steven looked at his watch and said, _____.

Name _____

Learning Checkpoint Chapters 1–4

> Read the paragraph. Circle the common nouns. Underline the verbs.

1. Lions live in prides. The lions in the pride help each other. Female lions hunt for food. They sneak through the tall grass. Male lions protect the cubs. They roar really loud! It scares predators.

> Circle each pronoun, reflexive pronoun, or indefinite pronoun in the sentences.

2. Rosa had to choose an animal for her report.

3. She wanted an animal no one else picked.

4. She asked her teacher, but she said, "Choose the animal yourself!"

5. Rosa made a list of animals for herself.

> Read each sentence. Look at the underlined word. Write **adjective** or **adverb** to name the part of speech.

6. The class presented their reports <u>yesterday</u>. _____

7. Everyone listened <u>quietly</u>. _____

8. Rosa picked the <u>mighty</u> lion. _____

9. It was an <u>interesting</u> report! _____

Learning Checkpoint Chapters 1–4

Read the sentences below. Write **S** if the sentence is a statement. Write **Q** if it is a question. Write **E** if it is an exclamation. Write **C** if it is a command.

10. Omar likes working in his garden. _____

11. Do you want to help? _____

12. Water the plants. _____

13. Watch out for the bee! _____

Combine each pair of sentences. Write the new sentence.

14. Lilies are a type of flower. Daisies are a type of flower.

_____

15. Omar weeded his garden. Omar watered his garden.

_____

16. The tomatoes are red. The tomatoes are tasty.

_____

Expand the simple sentence. Add more adjectives and/or adverbs.

17. Omar has a garden.

_____

_____

Learning Checkpoint Chapters 1–4

Read and proofread the paragraph. Underline each letter that should be a capital letter three times. Then, write the capital letter above it.

18.   in school today, ms. Wilson taught us about Katherine johnson.

katherine helped send the first man to the moon. she

did it by working as a computer! ms. wilson said

that means she did a lot of math. i guess math can

be exciting!

If the place, date, or holiday is written correctly, write a ✓ on the line. If it is not written correctly, rewrite it.

19.   juneteenth   _____

20.   August 26   _____

21.   west Virginia   _____

22.   Douglass Elementary   _____

23.   june 19   _____

24.   Earth Day   _____

Learning Checkpoint Chapters 1–4

Read each sentence. Add the correct end mark.

25. I have always wanted a dog

26. Dad said it's a lot of responsibility

27. Do you know what I got for my birthday

28. My very own puppy

Rewrite each sentence. Add commas where they are needed.

29. My dog is a puppy but she's already 50 pounds!

_____

_____

30. She's a Labrador Retriever and she likes to swim.

_____

_____

31. Labrador Retrievers come from Newfoundland Canada.

_____

_____

Add quotation marks around the exact words a speaker says. Underline the titles of books.

32. Do you like to read? asked Ari. I'm reading The Boxcar Children.

33. Yes! My favorite book is Dragons in a Bag, answered Kyra.

Chapter 5: Usage ••

Crafting good sentences relies on understanding how to use words correctly on their own and in relation to other words in the sentence. A good place to start is by practicing subject-verb agreement—making sure that a singular subject has a singular verb, or a plural subject has a plural verb.

Devote time as well to verbs and their tenses. While some verbs easily transform into past tense by adding *-ed*, many do not. Irregular verbs, like *eat/ate* or *draw/drew*, do not follow a simple pattern for changing tense. These are ones that students simply need to memorize.

A tricky skill, even for some adults, is learning when to use the pronouns *I* and *me*. Chapter 5 offers practice in using these pronouns.

Students will learn how to identify and show possession. Exercises for singular and plural possession give students practice with correct placement of the apostrophe so that they know if the *dogs' food* is food for one dog or more than one dog.

Skills Checklist ••

☐ Using subject-verb agreement

☐ Memorizing irregular verbs and their tenses

☐ Forming the past tense of verbs by adding *-ed*

☐ Using pronouns *I* and *me*

☐ Using a possessive pronoun before a noun or by itself

Helpful Definitions

subject: a word or group of words in a sentence that tells who or what performs the action expressed by the verb; Examples: *Kristina* likes raisins. *My dog* is friendly. *He* cried.

verb: an action word that tells what happens in a sentence; Examples: *jump, write, play*

irregular verb: a verb whose main parts are not formed according to the regular pattern; Examples: *go-went-gone, buy-bought-bought, drink-drank-drunk, sink-sank-sunk*

past tense: the form of a verb that shows that an action took place in the past; Examples: I *played* with my dog in the yard. My teacher *asked* me for my homework. The waiter *spilled* water all over the table.

pronoun: a word that takes the place of a noun; Examples: *they, her, we, it*

possessive pronoun: a word that shows that something belongs to the one referred to; Examples: That pen is *mine*. The bus is *ours*. This is *their* house.

Tools and Tips

How we use language depends on how we heard or learned language as infants. Some sentence structure comes naturally as we speak. Books offer opportunities to point out language choices the author makes to convey something. Songs, with their rhymes, help students internalize language structure. Other language rules have to be practiced. Practice tense shift and other usage rules through play. A game of *Simon Says* allows students to differentiate between tenses. "Simon says turn around" vs. "Simon says turned around."

Second grade is a year where language is still being misused. For example, your student may say, "I buyed the chips" instead of "I bought the chips." Model, rather than correct, your student. Respond with, "You bought these chips?" or similar to model correct verb tense.

Name _____

Lesson 5.1 Subject-Verb Agreement (Adding *s*)

When there is only one person or thing in the subject of the sentence, add **s** to the end of the **verb**.

    Caleb run**s** to the park.   Ms. Wheeler read**s** to us every day.

When there is more than one person or thing in the subject, or when using *you*, the verb does not end with *s*.

    The balloons float through the air.   You pull the string.

> **Write the correct verb from the parentheses ( ) to complete each sentence.**

1. Wade _____ a game for the family. (pick, picks)

2. He _____ the wheel. (spin, spins)

3. Wade _____ a picture on a big sheet of paper. (draw, draws)

4. Mom and Dad _____. (laugh, laughs)

5. Alicia _____ what the picture is. (know, knows)

6. She _____ the bell. (ring, rings)

7. Alicia and Wade _____ a good team. (make, makes)

Name _____

Lesson 5.1 Subject-Verb Agreement (Adding *s*)

1. The Andersons love___ game night.

2. Alicia choose___ the game.

3. She pick___ her favorite board game.

4. Mom, Dad, Alicia, and Wade roll___ the dice.

5. Wade take___ the first turn.

6. He move___ his piece four spaces.

7. Mom roll___ the dice.

8. Uh-oh! Mom lose___ her turn.

9. Mom never win___ this game!

Can you write two sentences using the verbs *play* and *plays*? Try it!

_____

_____

Lesson 5.2 Subject-Verb Agreement (Adding es)

Add **es** to **verbs** that end in *sh, ch, s, x,* and *z*.

Ellie brush**es** her teeth twice a day.   He miss**es** his old house.

When there is more than one person or thing in the subject, do not add *es* to the verb.

Mom and Gale stitch the holes in my quilt.

> Complete each sentence with the correct word from the parentheses ( ).

1. The bee _____ when it flies close

    to my ear. (buzz, buzzes)

2. Alexandra and Thomas _____ all

    the dishes after dinner. (wash, washes)

3. Manuel _____the ball to Ashley. (toss, tosses)

4. Noelle _____ for something special when she blows

    out her candles. (wish, wishes)

5. Liam _____the batter before he pours it in the pan.

    (mix, mixes)

Name _____

Lesson 5.2 Subject-Verb Agreement (Adding *es*)

Circle the verb in each sentence. If it is correct, make a ✓ on the line. If it is not correct, write the correct form. Then, find and circle each correct verb form in the puzzle. Words can be found across, down, and diagonally.

1. Mom and Dad relaxes on the weekends. _____

2. The snake hisses at the bird. _____

3. Liza catch the bus each morning. _____

4. Sean waxes his surfboard on the beach. _____

5. The red sports car pass the truck. _____

c	m	o	a	k	i	z	y	r	b
p	a	u	p	e	e	q	q	c	r
p	a	t	d	p	h	x	j	r	m
y	y	s	c	h	d	z	j	d	q
a	q	a	s	h	i	q	w	f	d
r	v	h	n	e	e	s	l	o	a
e	w	a	x	e	s	s	s	b	v
l	c	e	e	j	e	w	g	e	r
a	g	q	j	c	v	w	r	i	s
x	d	v	q	k	d	v	j	s	e

 Explain the rule for making a verb agree with a plural subject.

_____

_____

Name _____

Lesson 5.3 Irregular Verbs: *Am, Is, Are*

Some verbs do not show action. The words *am, is*, and ***are*** are all different forms of the verb **to be**.

Use **am** with *I*.
    I **am** happy.   I **am** behind the door.

Use **is** when there is only one person or thing.
    Tommy **is** my brother.   The sky **is** blue.

Use **are** with *you*.
    You **are** lucky.   You **are** my friend.

Use **are** when there is more than one person or thing.
    Bianca and Charley **are** at school.   They **are** in second grade.

> Write the correct verb from the parentheses ( ) to complete each sentence.

1. I _____ tall and strong.
       (is, am)

2. You _____ a great cook.
       (are, am)

3. Mike and Matt _____ twins.
           (is, are)

4. This soup _____ too spicy!
          (is, am)

5. All the girls in my class _____ present.
                    (is, are)

6. That doorknob _____ broken.
            (are, is)

Spectrum Language Arts **Grade 2**

Lesson 5.3 Irregular Verbs: *Am, Is, Are*

Read the diary entry. Cross out each incorrect verb. Then, write the correct verb above it.

Thursday, May 27

Dear Diary,

Victoria are my friend. She knows lots of jokes. Today, I told

her, "You am the funniest person I know! I are glad to be your

friend."

We is in a club together. Owen and Rachel is in the club, too.

We learn all kinds of jokes. Knock-knock jokes is my favorite.

Riddles am Victoria's favorite.

Owen are older than us. He am in third grade. He tells us all

the third-grade jokes. We spend a lot of time laughing!

Lesson 5.4 Irregular Verbs: *Has, Have*

Some verbs do not show action. The verb **to have** does not show action. **Has** and **have** are different forms of the verb *to have*.

Use **have** with *I* or *you*.
   I **have** six cats.   You **have** a bird.

Use **have** when there is more than one person or thing.
   We **have** a French lesson this afternoon.   They **have** a green car.
   Maureen and Ramon **have** brown hair.   The tree and plant **have** leaves.

Use **has** when there is only one person or thing.
   She **has** two braids.   Lex **has** a book about fossils.

> Complete each sentence with the correct verb form in parentheses ( ).

1.   Maple trees and oak trees _____ similar leaves.
                                              (has, have)

2.   A gingko tree _____ leaves that look like fans.
                                     (has, have)

3.   We _____ a large fir tree in the backyard.
                     (has, have)

4.   The Maddens _____ many trees that bloom in the spring.
                              (has, have)

5.   Lila _____ an enormous, old maple tree in the front yard.
                     (has, have)

Name _____

Lesson 5.4 Irregular Verbs: *Has, Have*

> Cross out the incorrect verb in each sentence. Then, write the correct verb above it.

1. Holly trees has shiny red berries.

2. You has a beautiful weeping willow tree.

3. An apple tree have plenty of fruit in autumn.

4. A mulberry tree have berries that birds love to eat.

5. Jaya and Chad has a swing in the old oak tree.

6. I has a piece of bark from the white birch tree.

7. Sparrows and chickadees has a nest in the elm tree.

 Explain why you would use the verb form *has* for the word *team*.

_____

_____

Lesson 5.5 Forming the Past Tense by Adding *ed*

Verbs in the present tense tell about things that are happening right now. Verbs in the **past tense** tell about things that already happened.

Add **ed** to most verbs to tell about the past.
    The foxes jump over the log. ————————→ The foxes jump**ed** over the log.

If the verb already ends in e, just add **d**.
    They hike two miles. ————————→ They hike**d** two miles.

> Complete each sentence with the past tense form of the verb in parentheses ( ).

1. Annie Smith Peck _____ to many countries. (travel)

2. In 1888 she _____ Mount Shasta in California. (climb)

3. She _____ to climb the Matterhorn one day. (hope)

4. Annie _____ a group called the American Alpine Club. (start)

5. She _____ the volcanoes of South America. (explore)

6. She _____ hard so she could climb in her spare time. (work)

Name _____

Lesson 5.5 Forming the Past Tense by Adding *ed*

Rewrite each sentence with the past tense form of the underlined verb.

1. Annie Smith Peck <u>climb</u> many mountains.

    _____

2. She <u>live</u> from 1850 until 1935.

    _____

3. Annie <u>show</u> the world how strong women can be.

    _____

    _____

4. She <u>want</u> to set records in climbing.

    _____

 Can you write a sentence about an accomplishment of a woman in your life? Try it! Use a regular past tense verb.

_____

_____

Lesson 5.6 Past Tense Verbs: *Was, Were*

The word **was** is the **past tense** form of *am* and *is*. Remember to use **was** only if there is one person or thing.

 I **was** tired.   The stove **was** hot.

The word **were** is the past tense form of *are*. Remember to use **were** if there is more than one person or thing.

 We **were** a team.   The monkeys **were** funny.

> Write **was** or **were** to complete each sentence.

Last Tuesday, my brother Benjamin _____ on TV. He

_____ at the park with his friend Allison. It _____

a sunny day. They _____ on the jungle gym. A

news reporter _____ at the park, too. She

_____ a reporter for Channel WBVA news. She asked people in

the park if the city should build a new pool. Benjamin and Allison

_____ excited about the interview. My family watched Benjamin

on the evening news. I _____

proud of my brother, the TV star!

Lesson 5.6 Past Tense Verbs: *Was, Were*

Rewrite each sentence in the past tense.

1. Ann is late for school.

_____

2. They are happy to see the bus.

_____

3. I am glad Brad wore the hat I gave him.

_____

4. You are on vacation.

_____

5. Mom and I are shopping for groceries.

_____

Can you write a sentence about something that is happening right now? Try it! Then, write the same sentence in the past tense.

_____

_____

_____

_____

Name _____

Lesson 5.7 Past Tense Verbs: *Had*

The past tense form of *have* and *has* is **had**.

Present Tense
I have four pets.
The flowers have red petals.
Hayden has short hair.

Past Tense
I **had** four pets.
The flowers **had** red petals.
Hayden **had** short hair.

Complete each sentence with *has*, *have*, or *had*. Use the tense in the parentheses ( ).

My bike _____ a horn and a scoop seat. (present)

My mom _____ a bike just like it when she was little. (past)

The wheels _____ shiny silver spokes. (present)

My mom's old bike _____ a bell, too. (past)

Spectrum Language Arts **Grade 2**

Name _____

Lesson 5.7 Past Tense Verbs: *Had*

Circle the verb in each sentence. If the verb is in the present tense, write **present**. If it is in the past tense, write **past**.

1. _____ The one-dollar bill has a picture of George Washington on it.

2. _____ I had four dollars in my piggybank.

3. _____ The twenty-dollar bill has a picture of Andrew Jackson on it.

4. _____ Greg and Devi had ten dollars to spend at the bookstore.

5. _____ My sister has eight dollars.

6. _____ My parents have a coin collection.

7. _____ Ian had a two-dollar bill.

Can you write a sentence about something you have? Try it! Then, write the same sentence in the past tense.

_____

_____

_____

_____

Lesson 5.8 Past Tense Verbs: *Went*

The past tense form of *go* and *goes* is **went**.

Present Tense
We go to the fair with our cousins.
Lorenzo goes to Florida.

Past Tense
We **went** to the fair with our cousins.
Lorenzo **went** to Florida.

Rewrite each sentence in the past tense.

1. We go to the store.

   _____

2. We go sledding with Miki and Ted.

   _____

3. Sanjay goes home at noon.

   _____

4. Rae goes to her singing lesson today.

   _____

Lesson 5.8 Past Tense Verbs: *Went*

Read the text. Cross out the verbs that are in the wrong tense. Write the correct verbs above them.

When my dad was little, his family goes to a cabin every summer. He loved

the little cabin in the woods. His cousins came to visit. Everyone goes swimming in

the lake. They go on long bike rides. They built forts in the woods. Grandma and

Grandpa go for long walks. Once the entire family came from miles away. They

go to a big family party on the beach.

Dad loved those summers in the woods.

Some day, he will take us to see the old cabin.

Explain what types of words in a text tell you what verb tense to use.

_____

_____

Lesson 5.9 Past Tense Verbs: *Saw*

The past tense form of *see* and *sees* is **saw**.

Present Tense
My mom sees me swimming.
They see the puppy every day.

Past Tense
My mom **saw** me swimming.
They **saw** the puppy every day.

Rewrite each sentence in the past tense.

1. We see raindrops on the leaves.

   _____

2. The dog sees the little girl on the hill.

   _____

3. Dad sees the tiny cut with his glasses.

   _____

4. The three birds see their mother.

   _____

5. Tess sees that movie three times.

   _____

6. Cam and Dillon see the hot air balloon.

   _____

   _____

Name _____

Lesson 5.9 Past Tense Verbs: *Saw*

> Read the paragraph. Cross out the verbs that are in the wrong tense. Write the correct verbs above them.

Last month, my aunt got married in Key West, Florida. We drove to the

wedding. We see many interesting things on our visit. My sister sees dolphins

playing in the water. Dad took us to Ripley's Believe It or Not Museum. We see

many strange and amazing things there. Later, we went to the Chicken Store. It

is a place that rescues chickens. We see dozens of chickens there. I did not know

Key West had so many homeless chickens!

Name _____

Lesson 5.10 Irregular Past Tense Verbs

An **irregular verb** does not follow the pattern of a regular verb when changing tense. It becomes a new word.

run → ran   sleep → slept   draw → drew

Complete each sentence with the correct irregular past tense verb in parentheses ( ).

1. Sal's mom _____ him a bedtime story.
    (tell, told, telled)

2. My teacher _____ me a nice letter.
    (wrote, write, writed)

3. Jalen's neighbor _____ him how to play pickleball.
    (teached, teach, taught)

4. Hoover _____ so fast after the squirrel.
    (ran, runned, run)

5. Last night my big brother _____ six pieces of pizza!
    (eat, eaten, ate)

6. Diego's book _____ off his desk onto his foot.
    (falled, fall, fell)

7. The plate _____ when Angel bumped it off the table.
    (breaked, broke, brake)

8. Mia and Jo _____ a jellyfish in the water.
    (feeled, felt, felted)

Lesson 5.10 Irregular Past Tense Verbs

Read each present tense verb. Find and write the matching irregular past tense verb from the box.

taught	ran	ate	grew	swam	sat
drove	sang	made	wrote	gave	took
saw	left	won	drank	built	knew

1. win _____

2. teach _____

3. leave _____

4. see _____

5. make _____

6. run _____

7. drink _____

8. know _____

9. eat _____

10. write _____

11. grow _____

12. swim _____

13. sit _____

14. drive _____

15. sing _____

16. give _____

17. take _____

18. build _____

Lesson 5.11 Pronouns *I* and *Me*

I and **me** are both **pronouns**. Pronouns are words that take the places of nouns. The pronouns *I* and *me* are used when the writer is talking about himself or herself.

> **I** took the bus downtown.   **I** bought a sandwich.
> The police officer waved to **me**.   The woman gave **me** a ticket.

When you are talking about yourself and another person, always put the other person first.

> Robyn and **I** left early.
> He gave the shells to Dexter and **me**.

> Read the clues to find out who wrote the sentences. Complete each sentence with the pronoun **I** or **me**.

1. _____ was born in New York in 1899.

2. My five brothers and sisters were older than _____.

3. My wife and _____ moved to a farm in Maine.

4. _____ loved to read, write, and do chores on the farm.

5. A spider in my barn gave _____ the idea for a children's story.

Who is the writer?

It is E. B. White, the famous author of the books *Charlotte's Web* and *Stuart Little*.

Lesson 5.11 Pronouns *I* and *Me*

Read each sentence. If the correct pronoun is used, write a √ on the line. If it is incorrect, write the correct pronoun on the line.

1. _____ Me went to the store yesterday.

2. _____ Chris and I are on the same baseball team.

3. _____ Is that package for I?

4. _____ My sister and me are going to the playground.

5. _____ I had a great time last year at the museum.

6. _____ Running is good for I.

7. _____ Dad and me took the subway downtown.

8. _____ Amina gave I an invitation to the party.

 Explain when you would use *you and me* and *you and I* in your writing.

_____

_____

_____

Lesson 5.12 Possessive Pronouns

Possessive pronouns show ownership.
   his hat   **her** shoes   **our** dog

Use these pronouns before a noun: *my, our, you, his, her, its, their*
   That is **my** bike.

Use these pronouns on their own: *mine, yours, ours, his, hers, theirs, its*
   That is **mine**.

> Rewrite each sentence using a pronoun from the box in place of the underlined word.

mine	yours	hers	his	ours

1. That is <u>her book</u>.

_____

2. This is <u>my pencil</u>.

_____

3. This hat is <u>your hat</u>.

_____

4. Fifi is <u>his cat</u>.

_____

5. That one is <u>our car</u>.

_____

Lesson 5.12 Possessive Pronouns

Underline the possessive pronoun(s) in each sentence.

1. That black dog is ours.

2. My pencil is broken. Pass me yours.

3. The brick house is theirs.

4. Roberto's flowers were healthier than mine.

5. Your car runs better than ours.

6. Sandra's parents are stricter than mine.

7. The gerbil is in its cage.

8. His name is Jovian.

Review Chapter 5

Circle the verb in each sentence. If it is correct, make a ✓ on the line. If it is not correct, write the correct verb on the line.

1. _____ The cricket hop across the field.

2. _____ Laurel catch a luna moth.

3. _____ The ant rushes toward the sticky candy wrapper.

4. _____ The ladybugs lands on the porch.

5. _____ The twins watches the praying mantis under the tree.

6. _____ The lightning bug flashes in the sky.

Complete each sentence with the correct verb in parentheses ( ).

7. Zach and Grace _____ a butterfly garden.
   (have, has)

8. The grasshopper and the beetle _____ green.
   (is, are)

9. The inchworm _____ under the large rock.
   (am, is)

10. I _____ lucky that the dragonfly landed on my arm.
    (am, are)

11. The fly _____ two wings.
    (have, has)

Review Chapter 5

Write the past tense form of the verb in parentheses ( ).

12. My grandpa _____ to many countries. (travel)

13. Last week I _____ a hot air balloon. (see)

14. My dog _____ so fast, I couldn't catch it. (run)

15. Our teacher _____ to the lunchroom to eat. (go)

16. My parents _____ happy to see my good grades. (are)

17. Diego _____ a hard time hearing the speaker. (has)

18. Martina _____ tennis for two hours after school. (play)

Complete each sentence with *I* or *me*.

19. Jake gave _____ a present for my birthday.

20. _____ washed my bike this weekend.

21. Sonya and _____ picked up trash at the park.

Underline the possessive pronoun in each sentence.

22. The mailbox on the left is theirs.

23. The blue sweatshirt is mine.

24. The dog lost its bone.

Chapter 6: Word Study

In Chapter 6, students will focus on studying how words have additional letters added or are shortened to convey different meanings.

Students naturally use contractions in casual conversations. Chapter 6 gives students practice in combining small words to form contractions. For example, the words *is* and *not* can be combined to make the contraction *isn't*. Students will learn how contractions can help their writing be less choppy and flow better.

While studying words in Chapter 6, students develop a strong knowledge of spelling patterns they can apply to their writing. Words change in their plural forms, sometime by adding *s*, *es*, or *ies* and sometimes changing completely or staying the same. Exercises in Chapter 6 will teach and support students in developing their spelling skills.

Skills Checklist

☐ Forming and using contractions with *not*

☐ Forming and using contractions with *am*, *is*, and *are*

☐ Forming and using contractions with *will*

☐ Learning the spellings of plural nouns (regular and irregular)

☐ Forming plural nouns with *s*, *es*, and *ies*

☐ Learning the spellings of irregular plural nouns

Helpful Definitions ●●●●●●●●●●●●●●●●●●●●●●●●●●●●●●●●●●●●●●

contraction: two words combined with an apostrophe; Examples: *I'd, wouldn't, won't, don't*

plural noun: a noun that refers to more than one person, place, thing, or idea; Examples: *students, eggs, houses, apples*

irregular plural noun: plural nouns that do not become plural by adding *s* or *es*; Examples: *man-men, woman-women, person-people, mouse-mice, party-parties*

Tools and Tips ●●

Involving students in word sorts is a helpful way to practice plurals. Write on index cards lists of nouns that would have an added s, added es, and added ies in their plural forms. Have your student choose a word and tell the plural word form. Have them place it in a pile. Continue with the other words and encourage your student to notice the words falling into the same piles and their common spelling patterns. Challenge your student by including several irregular plurals that change completely or stay the same.

Lesson 6.1 Contractions with *Not*

A **contraction** is a shorter way of saying or writing something. In a contraction, two words are joined and an **apostrophe** (') takes the place of the missing letters.

Many contractions are formed with the word ***not***. The apostrophe takes the place of the letter *o* in ***not***.

is not = **isn't**   are not = **aren't**
was not = **wasn't**   were not = **weren't**
does not = **doesn't**   did not = **didn't**
have not = **haven't**   cannot = **can't**

Read each sentence. Write the letter of the contraction that matches the underlined word or words.

1. _____ The cat and the mouse <u>are not</u> friends.   **a.**   can't

2. _____ They <u>cannot</u> get along.   **b.**   isn't

3. _____ They <u>have not</u> tried very hard, though.   **c.**   wasn't

4. _____ The cat <u>was not</u> friendly to the mouse.   **d.**   weren't

5. _____ The mouse <u>is not</u> kind to the cat.   **e.**   aren't

6. _____ I guess the cat and mouse <u>were not</u>   **f.**   haven't
meant to live happily ever after.

Lesson 6.1 Contractions with *Not*

Circle the word or words in each sentence you could change to a contraction. Rewrite the sentence using the contraction.

1. Mr. Irving Mouse cannot come out during the day.

   _____

2. He does not want to run into Miss Lola Cat.

   _____

3. Being chased is not his idea of a good time.

   _____

4. He did not think Lola would be so rude.

   _____

5. They are not going to be able to share this house.

   _____

Explain when a writer might and might not use contractions.

_____

_____

_____

Lesson 6.2 Contractions with *Am, Is, Are*

Some contractions are formed with the words *am*, *is*, and *are*. The apostrophe takes the place of the letter *a* in *am*, the *i* in *is*, and the *a* in *are*.

I am = **I'm**	you are = **you're**
we are = **we're**	they are = **they're**
she is = **she's**	he is = **he's**
it is = **it's**	

> Read the diary entry. Find and cross out words that can be replaced with a contraction. Write the contraction above the crossed out words.

Dear Diary,

I am going to my karate class on Saturday morning. It is a class for

beginners. Maria and Toby are taking karate too. They are in my class. Maria

learned some karate moves from her older brother. He is in a different class.

Maria knows how to do more kicks than anyone else. I think she is the best

student. Allan is our karate teacher. He is 39 years old. Allan has been doing

karate since he was five. He has a black belt. Maria, Toby, and I plan to take

lessons for a long time. We are going to get our black belts one day, too.

Name _____

Lesson 6.2 Contractions with *Am, Is, Are*

Complete each sentence with a contraction from the box.

| It's | We're | You're | She's | He's | They're |

1. I think Allan is a great teacher. _____ patient and funny.

2. Maria's mom comes to every class. _____ interested in what we learn.

3. Toby and Maria are cousins. _____ both part of the Tarrano family.

4. Maria, Toby, and I will get our yellow belts next month. _____ excited to move up a level.

5. I like karate class a lot. _____ a good way to exercise and make friends.

6. Do you think you would like to try karate? _____ welcome to come watch one of our classes.

Lesson 6.3 Contractions with *Will*

Many contractions are formed with pronouns and the verb **will**. An apostrophe (')
takes the place of the letters *wi* in **will**.

I will = **I'll**	it will = **it'll**
you will = **you'll**	we will = **we'll**
she will = **she'll**	they will = **they'll**
he will = **he'll**	

Read each sentence. Write the letter of the contraction that matches the underlined word or words.

1. _____ <u>I will</u> travel into space one day.

2. _____ A spaceship will take me there. <u>It will</u> move very fast.

3. _____ <u>You will</u> be my copilot.

4. _____ My sister, Eva, can come along, too. <u>She will</u> direct the spaceship.

5. _____ <u>We will</u> make many important discoveries.

6. _____ Our families can have a party when we return. <u>They will</u> be so proud!

a. She'll

b. We'll

c. I'll

d. They'll

e. You'll

f. It'll

Lesson 6.3 Contractions with *Will*

Read the newspaper article. Find and cross out the pairs of words that can be replaced with a contraction. Write the contraction above the words.

Hughes to Become Youngest Astronaut

Jasmine Hughes is only nine years old. She will be the first child to journey into space. Jasmine has been training since she was four. She will travel on the space shuttle Investigator. Six other astronauts will be in her crew. They will have to work well as a team. Darren Unger will be the commander. He will be the leader of the crew. They know their mission is important. It will help scientists learn more about the universe. The world will be able to watch the trip on TV. We will see history being made!

Name _____

Lesson 6.4 Plural Nouns with *s*

The word **plural** means more than one. To make most nouns plural, just add **s**.

one clock   ⟶ two clock**s**
one shirt   ⟶ three shirt**s**
one girl   ⟶ many girl**s**
one squirrel ⟶ six squirrel**s**

> Read the sentences. Complete each sentence with the plural form of the word in parentheses ( ).

1. There are five blue _____ on Greece's flag. (stripe)

2. China's flag has five _____. (star)

3. The two _____ in Denmark's flag are red and white. (color)

4. Some flags have small _____ on them. (picture)

5. Jamaica's flag has four _____. (triangle)

6. _____ are on the flags of many countries. (Moon)

Lesson 6.4 Plural Nouns with *s*

The words below are all things that are on state flags of the United States. Write the plural form of each word on the line. Then, fill in the puzzle with the plural forms.

Down

1. date _____

2. bird _____

3. flower _____

5. tree _____

Across

4. animal _____

6. word _____

7. star _____

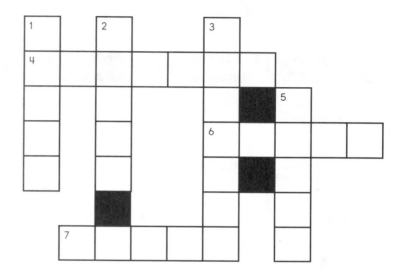

Can you write a sentence using two plural words from the puzzle? Try it!

_____

_____

Lesson 6.5 Plural Nouns with *es*

If a noun ends in *sh*, *ch*, *s*, or *x*, add **es** to make it **plural**.

one ax   ⟶   two ax**es**

one brush   ⟶   many brush**es**

one pouch   ⟶   six pouch**es**

one bus   ⟶   seven bus**es**

Rewrite each sentence with the plural form of the underlined words.

1. There are two <u>bunch</u> of grapes on the table.

   _____

2. The <u>peach</u> are in the basket.

   _____

3. Use the <u>box</u> to carry the oranges.

   _____

4. Please put the fruit in the yellow <u>dish</u>.

   _____

5. Each of the <u>class</u> will get to pick some berries.

   _____

Name _____

Lesson 6.6 Plural Nouns with *es*

Read the paragraphs. Cross out each incorrect noun and write the correct plural form above it.

We waited on the many bench outside of the school. Three bus picked us

up at nine o'clock. We went to Sunnyvale Apple Orchard. Mr. Krup gave us some

box to use. He showed us how to pick ripe apples. Many branch were heavy with

fruit. There were also some blueberry bush on the farm.

When we were done picking, the tractor brought us back to the farmhouse.

We ate our lunch at some picnic tables. Mrs. Krup gave

us glass of lemonade. Tomorrow, we'll make apple pies.

Can you think of a word that ends in *sh*, *ch*, *s*, or *x*, but does not add *es* to make it plural? Try it!

_____

_____

Lesson 6.6 Plural Nouns with *ies*

Singular nouns that end in a consonant and *y* become **plural** by dropping the *y* and adding **ies** to the end.

city ———→ cit**ies**   pony ———→ pon**ies**

> Write the plural form of each noun.

1. cherry _____

2. baby _____

3. penny _____

4. story _____

5. berry _____

6. family _____

7. sky _____

8. bunny _____

Spectrum Language Arts **Grade 2**

Lesson 6.6 Plural Nouns with *ies*

Color the leaf if the plural form of the word is formed by dropping the *y* and adding ies.

Name _____

Lesson 6.7 Irregular Plural Nouns

Some plural nouns do not follow the rules you have learned. To form the plurals of these nouns, do not add s or es. Instead, the word changes. Here are some examples of **irregular plural nouns**.

one man ⟶ three **men**
one woman ⟶ four **women**
one foot ⟶ two **feet**
one goose ⟶ five **geese**
one child ⟶ ten **children**
one tooth ⟶ many **teeth**
one mouse ⟶ twenty **mice**

Some nouns do not change at all in their plural forms.

one deer ⟶ many **deer**
one moose ⟶ nine **moose**
one fish ⟶ sixty **fish**
one sheep ⟶ one hundred **sheep**

Match each singular noun to its plural form.

one tooth   nine deer

one child   four feet

one foot   twelve mice

one goose   several teeth

one deer   lots of children

one mouse   two men

one man   seven geese

Name _____

Lesson 6.7 Irregular Plural Nouns

Write the plural form of each word. Then, find and circle each plural word in the puzzle. Words can be found across and down.

1. woman _____

2. fish _____

3. moose _____

4. mouse _____

5. foot _____

6. sheep _____

7. child _____

8. tooth _____

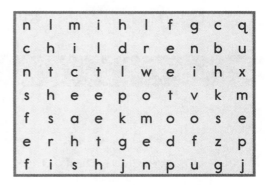

n	l	m	i	h	l	f	g	c	q
c	h	i	l	d	r	e	n	b	u
n	t	c	t	l	w	e	i	h	x
s	h	e	e	p	o	t	v	k	m
f	s	a	e	k	m	o	o	s	e
e	r	h	t	g	e	d	f	z	p
f	i	s	h	j	n	p	u	g	j

Write two sentences. Use the plural form of at least one word from the box in each sentence.

| foot | man | fish | mouse | deer | goose |

_____

_____

Lesson 6.8 Comparative Adjectives

Adjectives are words that describe nouns.

Add **er** to an adjective to compare two nouns. Add **est** to an adjective to compare three or more nouns.

    Rosa is tall.   Jill is tall**er**.   Bethany is tall**est**.

> Circle the correct adjective in parentheses to complete each sentence.

1. Mount Everest is the (highest, higher) mountain.

2. The (tall, tallest) waterfall in the world is Angel Falls in Venezuela.

3. The Nile River is (longest, longer) than the Amazon River.

4. The Pacific Ocean is (deeper, deep) than the Indian Ocean.

5. It is the world's (deeper, deepest) ocean.

Name _____

Lesson 6.8 Comparative Adjectives

Write the missing adjectives in each row.

1. young _____ youngest

2. _____ faster fastest

3. dark _____ _____

4. hard harder _____

5. new _____ newest

6. _____ shorter _____

7. small _____ _____

8. kind _____ kindest

Can you compare three things around you? Write the adjectives you would use.

_____

_____

Lesson 6.9 Compound Words

Write a word from the box on each line to complete each compound word.

stack	bells	fast	end	rise
parents	yard	field	house	wood

1. My grand_____ live on a small farm.

2. They both wake up before sun_____.

3. Grandmother makes their break_____.

4. She also feeds the animals in the barn_____.

5. Grandfather must keep the inside of the farm_____ tidy.

6. He must also chop and stack fire_____.

7. He must plow the corn_____.

8. I like the sound of the cow_____ ringing in the pasture.

9. I really enjoy jumping into the hay_____.

10. I enjoy visiting for the week_____.

Name _____

Lesson 6.9 Compound Words

Draw lines to connect the words that make compound words.

1. note   plane

air   drop

sun   book

rain   light

2. basket   ball

any   time

down   fish

gold   stairs

3. him   to

jelly   self

in   fish

horse   shoe

4. every   store

ginger   way

drive   bread

drug   one

Review Chapter 6

In each sentence, circle the word or words you can make into a contraction. Then, write the contraction.

1. Kumar and Meg have not painted a mural before. _____

2. They cannot wait to begin. _____

3. We will buy the paints and brushes tonight. _____

4. I am going to a movie tonight. _____

5. Jamal said he is too tired to play outside. _____

6. They are leaving for the museum in minutes. _____

Read each phrase. Circle the correct plural form.

7. one peach   two peaches   two peachs

8. one dinosaur   fifty dinosaur   fifty dinosaurs

9. one balloon   a few balloons   a few balloones

10. one kiss   three kiss's   three kisses

11. one fly   too many flies   too many flys

12. one cherry   six cherrys   six cherries

Review Chapter 6

Write the irregular plural noun for each word.

1. one child   many _____

2. one foot   two _____

3. one person   ten _____

4. one tooth   four _____

5. one deer   three _____

6. one woman   five _____

Write the correct form of the adjective from the parentheses ( ) to complete each sentence.

7. Diamonds are the _____ stone. (hard)

8. The gray rock is _____ than the black rock. (smooth)

9. The _____ rock in my collection has a fern fossil. (old)

10. The edges of the fossil are _____ than the other rocks. (rough)

11. My _____ rock is less than half an inch long. (small)

Draw lines to connect the words to make compound words.

snow   paper

rain   way

news   drop

drive   ball

In Chapter 7, students will focus on the meanings of words as they relate to other words. Exercises will show students that words not only have meaning on their own, in isolation, but that words often have relationships with other words. Sometimes two different words have the same or similar meanings (synonyms), and using colorful synonyms in writing adds interest and pizzazz. Using words that are opposites (antonyms) in writing can add unexpected drama or contrast.

Homophones and homographs can often confuse readers and writers. It's important for students to know that words can sound alike but have different spellings and meanings, like *new/knew* and *here/hear* (homophones), and that words can be spelled the same but mean different things, such as *fair/fair* and *watch/watch* (homographs). The key to correctly identifying the correct word and meaning for homophones and homographs is understanding the context of the sentence.

When learning new words, teach students that words and their meanings can be altered by adding prefixes and suffixes to them. These short add-ons to the beginnings and endings of base words can take a word like *help* and turn it into a descriptive adjective, such as *helpful* or *unhelpful*. Exercises in Chapter 7 will teach students to identify a base word and its meaning.

Skills Checklist ••••••••••••••••••••••••••••••••••••••

- [ ] Identifying and using synonyms and antonyms

- [ ] Using closely-related verbs and adjectives

- [ ] Identifying and using homophones and homographs

- [ ] Identifying base words

Helpful Definitions

synonym: a word that has the same or nearly the same meaning as another word; Examples: *shut, close; big, large; happy, glad*

antonym: a word, often an adjective, that means the opposite of another word; Examples: *hot, cold; short, tall; loud, quiet*

homophone: one of two or more words that have the same pronunciation but different spellings and different meanings; Examples: *to, too, two; pair, pear; write, right; won, one*

homograph: one of two or more words that have the same spelling but different meanings and sometimes different pronunciations; Examples: *wind, wind; bass, bass; live, live*

base word: a stand-alone word found within a word that has a prefix and/or suffix; Examples: re*teach*, *teach*able, *teach*er

prefix: a word part added to the beginning of a base word that changes the meaning of the word; Examples: *re*teach, *un*wind

suffix: a word part added to the end of a base word that changes the meaning of the word; Examples: sing*er*, teach*er*

Tools and Tips

Have your student grab a highlighter and get ready to go on a word hunt. Use a piece of text your student wrote or an article you've printed. Have your student find words that have affixes. Have them highlight the root word.

The same can be done with antonyms, synonyms, homophones, and homographs. For example, finding the words *to, two*, and *too* in context can help reinforce their use in your student's writing. Identifying synonyms and antonyms in context can lead to a discussion about different words to use to convey stronger feeling or more description.

Lesson 7.1 Synonyms

Synonyms are words that have the same, or almost the same, meanings. Synonyms can help you become a better writer by making your writing less repetitive and more interesting to read. Here are some examples of synonyms.

little, small	quick, fast	easy, simple
begin, start	under, below	laugh, giggle

> Match each word in the first column to its synonym in the second column. Write the letter of the synonym on the line.

1. _____ beautiful   **a.** enjoy

2. _____ boat   **b.** toss

3. _____ like   **c.** happy

4. _____ tired   **d.** ship

5. _____ grin   **e.** pal

6. _____ glad   **f.** sleepy

7. _____ friend   **g.** pretty

8. _____ throw   **h.** smile

Explain when you might use synonyms in your writing.

_____

_____

Lesson 7.1 Synonyms

Read the sentences. Each underlined word has a synonym in the box. Write the synonym on the line at the end of the sentence.

giggled	bugs	hop	dad	pick	liked	terrific

1. Malik needed to <u>choose</u> a topic for his report.   _____

2. He and his <u>father</u> sat down at the computer.   _____

3. Malik <u>enjoyed</u> using the Internet for school
    projects.   _____

4. All of a sudden, he had a <u>great</u> idea.   _____

5. "I think I'm going to do my report on <u>insects</u>,"
    Malik told his dad.   _____

6. Malik and Dad watched a cartoon cricket <u>jump</u>
    across the computer screen.   _____

7. Malik <u>laughed</u> when the cricket stopped
    and waved.   _____

Name _____

Lesson 7.2 Antonyms

An **antonym** is a word that means the opposite of another word. Here are some examples of antonyms.

big, little   old, young   happy, sad

first, last   right, wrong   never, always

Circle the antonyms in each sentence.

1. The tall bottle is next to the short can.

2. Kent wore his new shirt with his favorite pair of old jeans.

3. I thought the quiz would be hard, but it was easy.

4. Did Miranda smile or frown when she saw you?

5. One pair of shoes is too tight, and one pair is too loose.

6. Open the cupboard, take out the cereal, and close the door.

7. It was hot outside, but it will be cold tomorrow.

8. Stephen was the first person in line and the last person to leave.

9. Would you rather go in the morning or night?

Explain when you might use antonyms in your writing.

_____

_____

Lesson 7.2 Antonyms

Read each word. Write an antonym for each word that fits in the spaces. Then, find and circle the antonyms in the puzzle. Words can be found across and down.

1. yell   __ __ __ __ __ __

2. yes   __ __

3. pull   __ __ __ __

4. love   __ __ __ __

5. empty   __ __ __ __

6. over   __ __ __ __ __

7. win   __ __ __ __

8. down   __ __

t	o	i	j	u	u	o	y	d	z
b	x	p	e	n	k	u	l	q	n
w	p	a	x	d	f	w	o	k	u
g	u	j	d	e	y	t	s	c	i
n	s	p	t	r	y	s	e	t	c
o	h	w	h	i	s	p	e	r	t
e	p	i	w	t	h	e	b	u	p
s	n	j	z	j	a	g	b	i	j
n	o	y	d	i	t	r	k	n	t
j	f	u	l	l	e	l	v	f	l

Name _____

Lesson 7.3 Closely-Related Verbs and Adjectives

Some **verbs** can be synonyms or have almost the same meanings. It is the **shades of meaning** a writer uses to help a reader understand what is happening.

Picture what a reader would see in their mind before choosing the best verb.

Ben **tosses** the ball to his teammate.

Ben **throws** the ball to his teammate.

Ben **hurls** the ball to his teammate.

> Circle the best verb to complete each sentence.

1. The lioness _____ at its prey.
   peeked   looked   stared

2. _____ up the stairs to me when you arrive.
   Speak   Shout   Mutter

3. I was late to class, so I had to _____.
   sprint   jog   walk

4. The stuntwoman _____ over the car in the movie scene.
   hopped   leaped   jumped

Name _____

Lesson 7.3 Closely-Related Verbs and Adjectives

Some **adjectives** can be synonyms or have almost the same meanings. It is the **shades of meaning** a writer uses to help a reader understand how something is described.

Picture what a reader would see in their mind before choosing the best adjective.
   We admired the **pretty** colors of the sunset.
   We admired the **beautiful** colors of the sunset.
   We admired the **gorgeous** colors of the sunset.

> Read each list of adjectives. Rewrite the list in the order described.

1. hot, warm, burning

least to greatest heat:

_____

_____

_____

2. poor, fair, great

least to greatest quality:

_____

_____

_____

3. content, joyful, happy

least to greatest feeling:

_____

_____

_____

4. wet, soaked, soggy

least to greatest amount of moisture:

_____

_____

_____

Lesson 7.4 Homophones

Homophones are words that sound alike but have different spellings and meanings. Here are some examples of homophones.

to = toward	We went **to** the gym.
to (use with a verb)	Dennis wants **to** skate.
two = the number that comes after one	Give the dog **two** biscuits.
too = also	We will go too.
too = very; more than enough	Lindy is **too** young to go.
by = next to	The bag is **by** the door.
bye = good-bye	Karim waved and said **bye**.
buy = to purchase something	I will **buy** three pears.
right = the opposite of wrong	That is the **right** answer.
write = to record your words	**Write** a report about the book.

Complete each sentence with the correct homophone.

1. I would like _____ see Pinocchio on ice. (to, too)

2. My sister wants to go, _____. (two, too)

3. Mom said she will try to _____ tickets tonight. (bye, buy)

4. I am going to _____ about the show in my diary. (write, right)

Name _____

Lesson 7.4 Homophones

Read the poster. Cross out each incorrect homophone. Then, write the correct homophone above it.

Come see Pinocchio on Ice!

This show is to much fun to miss. Make the write choice, and you'll

be glad you came two see these skaters.

The ice rink is downtown buy the theater.

By two tickets and get one free!
March 10—March 15

Can you write a sentence that uses both *right* and *write*? Try it!

_____

_____

Lesson 7.5 Homographs

Homographs are words that are spelled the same but have different meanings. You must read a sentence carefully to know which meaning a writer wants to use.

Casey got a baseball **bat** and a mitt for his birthday.
(a wooden stick used in baseball)

The brown **bat** eats about 2,000 insects a night.
(a small, flying mammal)

Read the dictionary entry for the word *cold*. Circle the form of the word as it is used in each sentence.

cold *adj.* having a low temperature; not warm

cold *noun* an illness that often includes a cough and a runny nose; a state of low temperature

1. It will be cold but sunny on Saturday.

    a. cold *adj.*   **b. cold** *noun*

2. I prefer warm meals more than cold meals.

    a. cold *adj.*   **b. cold** *noun*

3. Destiny caught a cold from her brother.

    a. cold *adj.*   **b. cold** *noun*

4. The cold water made us shiver.

    a. cold *adj.*   **b. cold** *noun*

Name _____

Lesson 7.5 Homographs

Look at the underlined words. Choose the definition that matches the way the word is used. Write the letter of that definition on the line.

1. _____ Airplanes <u>fly</u> at amazing speeds.

   a. a small insect with two wings   **b.** to move through the air

2. _____ The <u>leaves</u> were red, gold, and brown.

   a. parts of a tree or a plant   **b.** goes away

3. _____ May I <u>pet</u> your cat?

   a. an animal that lives with people   **b.** to touch lightly or stroke

4. _____ The Krugers did not <u>watch</u> the entire movie.

   a. view or look at   **b.** a small clock worn on the wrist

5. _____ Keely will <u>train</u> her puppy to roll over.

   a. to teach something by doing it over and over   **b.** a long line of cars that run on a track

Explain the difference between a homophone and a homograph.

_____

_____

_____

_____

Lesson 7.6 Base Words

A **base word** is the main part of a word separate from a prefix or suffix. It can stand alone on its own.

    un**kind**   **kind**ness

Sometimes, a letter is added to or dropped from the base word before adding a prefix or suffix.

    careful   **car**ing (drop the e)

> Draw a line between each prefix and base word or base word and suffix. The first one has been done for you.

1. un|lock

2. lovely

3. rewrite

4. reread

5. bravest

6. skipping

7. disappear

8. singer

9. preview

10. visitor

Can you write a word that has both a prefix and a suffix? Try it! Underline the base word.

_____

_____

Lesson 7.6 Base Words

Read each sentence. Underline the word that has a prefix or suffix. Write its base word on the line.

1. The preview of the movie was funny.

    _____

2. That bunny is adorable.

    _____

3. We will have to reschedule the trip.

    _____

4. Julian was careful with his aunt's new car.

    _____

5. You must have placed the papers on your desk.

    _____

6. Ms. Prim's comment to Shayla was thoughtless.

    _____

7. The boys disagree about how to play the game.

    _____

Review Chapter 7

> Read each pair of sentences. If the underlined words are synonyms, write **S** on the line. If they are antonyms, write **A** on the line.

1. _____ Colby's puppet had <u>dark</u> hair.

   Nina's puppet had <u>light</u> hair.

2. _____ <u>First</u>, Colby painted a face on his puppet.

   The <u>last</u> thing Nina did was button her puppet's dress.

3. _____ Nina tied a <u>little</u> bow in her puppet's hair.

   Colby's puppet had a <u>small</u> frog in its pocket.

4. _____ "You did a <u>great</u> job painting your puppet's face," said Nina.

   "I think your puppet is <u>terrific</u>," said Colby.

> Write a synonym and an antonym for each word.

5. big   _____   _____

6. fast   _____   _____

> Read the paragraph. Circle the correct homophones from the parentheses ( ).

When I leave for school, I say (buy, bye) to my little sister. She wishes she could go (to, two) school, (two, too), but she is not old enough. We are going to make a pretend school for her at home. My parents said they will (by, buy) us a chalkboard. We will put it (by, bye) the desk and the (too, two) small chairs. I will teach Melissa how to (write, right). She already knows the (write, right) way to make all the letters. She can't wait for school (to, too) start!

Review Chapter 7

Circle the correct meaning of each underlined word.

7.   The <u>leaves</u> are starting to change color.

parts of a tree   goes away

8.   I learned how to use a <u>bow</u> and arrow at summer camp.

to bend over   piece of wood used to shoot arrows

9.   She had a <u>tear</u> sliding down her cheek.

a rip   a drop that comes from an eye

10.   The river <u>winds</u> through the valley.

gusts of air   to turn or curve

Separate each word into its parts.

		Prefix	Base Word	Suffix
11.	grateful	_____	_____	_____
12.	misspell	_____	_____	_____
13.	rewrite	_____	_____	_____
14.	unhappy	_____	_____	_____
15.	endless	_____	_____	_____

Name _____

Learning Checkpoint Chapters 5–7

Circle the verb in each sentence. If it is correct, write a ✓ on the line. If it is not correct, write the correct form of the verb on the line.

1. I likes camping. _____

2. We roast marshmallows on the fire. _____

3. My sister tell a scary story. _____

4. I ask for a funny one! _____

Circle the correct verb to complete each sentence.

5. I (is, am) excited to go hiking.

6. Do you (has, have) your backpack ready?

Rewrite each sentence in the past tense.

7. I hike in Yellowstone National Park.

_____

8. It is the first national park in the US.

_____

Name _____

Learning Checkpoint Chapters 5–7

Dad's Tomato Sauce

Ingredients | Directions

Circle the two words in each sentence you could combine to make a contraction. Then, rewrite the sentence using the contraction.

9. I have not cooked my dad's sauce before.

_____

10. I am excited to learn!

_____

Write the correct plural form of each underlined word.

11. I looked at the list of <u>ingredient</u>. _____

12. We needed more <u>tomato</u>! _____

13. My dad tells <u>story</u> of cooking with his dad. _____

14. The <u>man</u> in my family love to cook! _____

Write the other forms of the adjectives.

15. _____ smaller _____

16. old _____ _____

Learning Checkpoint Chapters 5–7

Rewrite the underlined words in each sentence as a compound word.

17. My <u>grand father</u> was a great cook. _____

18. He wrote his recipes in a <u>note book</u>. _____

Read each pair of sentences. If the underlined words are synonyms, write *S* on the line. If they are antonyms, write *A* on the line.

19. _____ Hasan likes <u>warm</u> weather. Mai likes <u>cold</u> weather.

20. _____ Hasan <u>loves</u> the beach. Mai <u>likes</u> the mountains.

21. _____ Hasan thinks the snow is <u>pretty</u>. Mai thinks it is <u>beautiful</u>.

22. _____ Hasan hopes winter will be over <u>fast</u>! Mai hopes it goes by <u>slow</u>.

Circle the correct homophone to complete each sentence.

23. I have to (write, right) a story for class.

24. It is (do, due) next week.

25. My story will be about (too, two) dragons.

26. I can't wait (two, to) read it!

Learning Checkpoint Chapters 5–7

Write a sentence using each meaning of the word *wind.*

27. _____

_____

28. _____

_____

Read each sentence. Underline the word that has a prefix or suffix. Write its base word on the line.

29. Did you misplace your backpack?

_____

30. I am grateful for your help.

_____

31. That is the smallest kitten I have ever seen!

_____

32. Can you reuse that water bottle?

_____

Final Test

Read the sentences. Circle the nouns. Underline the verbs.

1. Bo and Malia play outside.

2. Bo throws a ball.

3. Malia swings on the rope.

4. Bo waves to a friend.

Read the paragraph. Circle each pronoun, reflexive pronoun, and indefinite pronoun.

5.   Harper practices playing her guitar. She is going to play in front of everyone

for the school talent show! Her brother helps her practice. They play together.

Harper tells him she is nervous. He says, "Believe in yourself! You will be great."

Read each sentence. If the underlined word is an adjective, write *adj.* on the line. If it is an adverb, write *adv.* on the line.

6. Malik is a <u>beautiful</u> singer. _____

7. <u>Tomorrow</u>, he will sing in the talent show. _____

8. I will <u>happily</u> listen to him! _____

9. It's going to be the <u>best</u> talent show. _____

Name _____

Final Test

Read the sentences. Write **S** if the sentence is a statement. Write **Q** if it is a question. Write **E** if it is an exclamation. Write **C** if it is a command.

10. Darren reads the cookie recipe. _____

11. Mix in the chocolate chips. _____

12. Did he add enough chocolate? _____

13. You can never have too much! _____

Combine each pair of sentences. Write the word you would use to combine them.

14. Darren needs butter for the cookies. Darren needs flour for the cookies.

Darren needs butter _____ flour for the cookies.

15. Darren added the ingredients. Darren mixed the ingredients.

Darren added _____ mixed the ingredients.

16. The cookies were gooey. The cookies were delicious.

The cookies were gooey _____ delicious.

Expand the sentence with more adjectives and/or adverbs.

17. Darren bakes cookies.

_____

Final Test

Rewrite each sentence. Use correct capitalization and punctuation.

18. mr. nu told us about a special dog named bobi

_____

19. bobi lived in portugal and was very old

_____

20. how old was bobi? aria asked

_____

21. mr. nu said can you believe he was 31

_____

Rewrite each place, date, or holiday with correct capitalization.

22. fourth of july _____

23. chicago, illinois _____

24. august _____

25. labor day _____

26. february 2, 2023 _____

27. jupiter _____

Final Test

Rewrite each phrase as a possessive.

28. the tail of the cat _____

29. the eyes of the boy _____

30. the shell of a turtle _____

31. the wheel of a car _____

Rewrite each phrase. Use an abbreviation in place of the underlined word.

32. <u>Monday</u>, July 14 _____

33. <u>Doctor</u> Sanchez _____

34. <u>Mister</u> Taylor _____

35. <u>January</u> 1 _____

Rewrite each sentence. Add commas where they are needed.

36. Dad is going to the store but he has to write a list first.

_____

37. We need bread fruit and peanut butter.

_____

38. The grocery store is in Portland Maine.

_____

Final Test

Complete each sentence with the pronoun *I* or *me*.

39. _____ like to paint.

40. My mom taught _____.

41. My mom and _____ paint together sometimes.

42. _____ hope to be as good as she is one day!

Underline the possessive pronoun in each sentence.

43. Is that book yours?

44. If you forgot your pencil, you can use mine.

45. The cat didn't like its collar.

46. Did you bring that bag of ours?

Circle the present tense verb in each sentence. If it agrees with the subject, write a ✓ on the line. If it does not agree, write the correct verb on the line.

47. Zara look for her raincoat. _____

48. Her parents tells her to hurry up. _____

49. She checks behind the door. _____

50. She find her raincoat! _____

Final Test

Complete each sentence with the correct past tense form of the verb in parentheses ( ).

51. Maya Angelou _____ an excellent writer. (is, was)

52. She _____ books and poems. (wrote, writes)

53. Maya _____ records and made history. (breaks, broke)

54. She _____ a great mind! (has, had)

Read the paragraph. Complete each sentence with the plural form of the word in parentheses ( ).

55.   We spotted _____ (dolphin) out in the water. A

bunch of _____ (family) gathered to see. My sister told

me they blow _____ (bubble). It helps them catch

_____ (fish) to eat! We jumped in the

_____ (wave). My sister splashed me. She said she was

pretending to use her _____ (fin)!

Final Test

Match each sentence to the contraction that takes the place of the underlined words.

56. <u>We will</u> come to the movies.

    a. You're

57. <u>You are</u> getting popcorn.

    b. We'll

58. I <u>have not</u> got my ticket yet.

    c. haven't

Rewrite each sentence. If there is an **A** after the sentence, use an antonym for the underlined word. If there is an **S**, use a synonym.

59. I want to build a tree house in a great, <u>small</u>, tree. **A**

_____

60. I <u>hate</u> heights, so a tree house would be perfect! **A**

_____

61. I could invite my <u>pals</u> to my tree house to play. **S**

_____

62. It would make me so <u>cheerful</u>! **S**

_____

Final Test

For each word, write its base word on the line.

63. redo _____ **64.** displease _____

65. teacher _____ **66.** untie _____

67. cutest _____ **68.** pretest _____

Write a sentence for each homophone: *to*, *too*, and *two*.

69. _____

_____

70. _____

_____

71. _____

_____

Answer Key

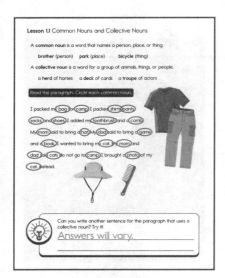

Lesson 1.1 Common Nouns and Collective Nouns

A **common noun** is a word that names a person, place, or thing.

brother (person)   park (place)   bicycle (thing)

A **collective noun** is a word for a group of animals, things, or people.

a **herd** of horses   a **deck** of cards   a **troupe** of actors

Read the paragraph. Circle each common noun.

I packed my (bag) for (camp) I packed (shirts) (pants) (socks) and (shoes) I added my (toothbrush) and a (comb). My (mom) said to bring a (hat). My (dad) said to bring a (game) and a (book). I wanted to bring my (cat). My (mom) and (dad) said (cats) do not go to (camp). I brought a (photo) of my (cat) instead.

Can you write another sentence for the paragraph that uses a collective noun? Try it!

Answers will vary.

page 8

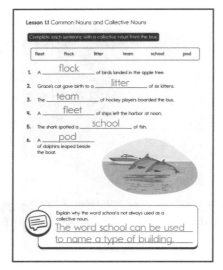

Lesson 1.1 Common Nouns and Collective Nouns

Complete each sentence with a collective noun from the box.

fleet	flock	litter	team	school	pod

1. A _____flock_____ of birds landed in the apple tree.

2. Grace's cat gave birth to a _____litter_____ of six kittens.

3. The _____team_____ of hockey players boarded the bus.

4. A _____fleet_____ of ships left the harbor at noon.

5. The shark spotted a _____school_____ of fish.

6. A _____pod_____ of dolphins leaped beside the boat.

Explain why the word *school* is not always used as a collective noun.

The word school can be used to name a type of building.

page 9

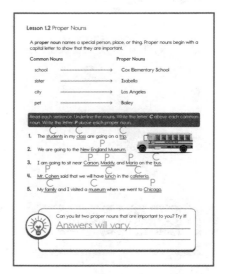

Lesson 1.2 Proper Nouns

A **proper noun** names a special person, place, or thing. Proper nouns begin with a capital letter to show that they are important.

Common Nouns	Proper Nouns
school	→ Cox Elementary School
sister	→ Isabella
city	→ Los Angeles
pet	→ Bailey

Read each sentence. Underline the nouns. Write the letter C above each common noun. Write the letter P above each proper noun.

1. The students in my class are going on a trip.
2. We are going to the New England Museum.
3. I am going to sit near Carson, Maddy, and Maria on the bus.
4. Mr. Cohen said that we will have lunch in the cafeteria.
5. My family and I visited a museum when we went to Chicago.

Can you list two proper nouns that are important to you? Try it!

Answers will vary.

page 10

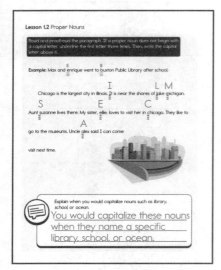

Lesson 1.2 Proper Nouns

Read and proofread the paragraph. If a proper noun does not begin with a capital letter, underline the first letter three times. Then, write the capital letter above it.

Example: Max and enrique went to buxton Public Library after school.

Chicago is the largest city in illinois. It is near the shores of lake michigan. Aunt suzanne lives there. My sister, ellie, loves to visit her in chicago. They like to go to the museums. Uncle alex said I can come visit next time.

Explain when you would capitalize nouns such as *library, school*, or *ocean*.

You would capitalize these nouns when they name a specific library, school, or ocean.

page 11

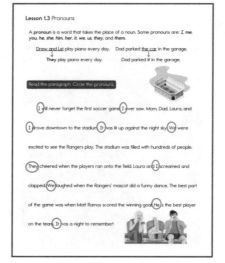

Lesson 1.3 Pronouns

A **pronoun** is a word that takes the place of a noun. Some pronouns are: *I, me, you, he, she, him, her, it, we, us, they,* and *them.*

Drew and Lei play piano every day.   Dad parked the car in the garage.
They play piano every day.   Dad parked it in the garage.

Read the paragraph. Circle the pronouns.

(I) will never forget the first soccer game (I) ever saw. Mom, Dad, Laura, and (I) drove downtown to the stadium. (It) was lit up against the night sky. (We) were excited to see the Rangers play. The stadium was filled with hundreds of people. (They) cheered when the players ran onto the field. Laura and (I) screamed and clapped. (We) laughed when the Rangers' mascot did a funny dance. The best part of the game was when Matt Ramos scored the winning goal. (He) is the best player on the team. (It) was a night to remember!

page 12

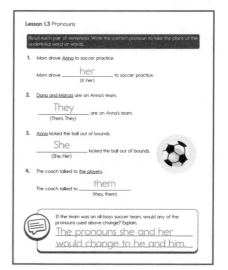

Lesson 1.3 Pronouns

Read each pair of sentences. Write the correct pronoun to take the place of the underlined word or words.

1. Mom drove Anna to soccer practice.

   Mom drove _____her_____ to soccer practice.
   (it, her)

2. Dana and Marcia are on Anna's team.

   _____They_____ are on Anna's team.
   (Them, They)

3. Anna kicked the ball out of bounds.

   _____She_____ kicked the ball out of bounds.
   (She, Her)

4. The coach talked to the players.

   The coach talked to _____them_____.
   (they, them)

If the team was an all-boys soccer team, would any of the pronouns used above change? Explain.

The pronouns she and her would change to he and him.

page 13

Answer Key

Lesson 1.4 Reflexive Pronouns

Reflexive pronouns are object pronouns that end in *-self* or *-selves* . They are used when the subject and object of a sentence are the same. Some reflexive pronouns are: *myself, yourself, himself, herself, itself, ourselves,* and *themselves.*

I can tie my shoes all by **myself**.   Do you talk to **yourself**?

Complete each sentence with a reflexive pronoun.

1. Carlos finished the Super Sundae ___himself___ .
2. I tied my sneakers all by ___myself___ .
3. Jill and Charlie made ___themselves___ a snack.
4. Angie finished the project ___herself___ .
5. Did that glass move ___itself___ ?
6. My brother and I cleaned the kitchen ___ourselves___ .

Can you write a sentence using the reflexive pronoun yourself? Try it!
___Answers will vary.___

page 14

Lesson 1.4 Reflexive Pronouns

In the situation below, Kyle's older sister is in charge of checking off the chore chart before school. Complete their conversation with reflexive pronouns.

Did you take out the garbage?

Yes, I did it ___myself___ .

Did Manny make his bed?

Yes. He did it ___himself___ .

Did you and Manny fold the laundry?

Yes, we did it ___ourselves___ .

Did you make me breakfast?

Ugh. Make it ___yourself___ !

page 15

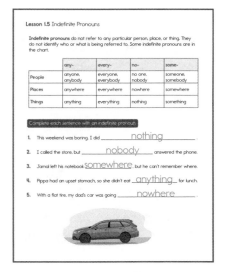

Lesson 1.5 Indefinite Pronouns

Indefinite pronouns do not refer to any particular person, place, or thing. They do not identify who or what is being referred to. Some indefinite pronouns are in the chart.

	any-	every-	no-	some-
People	anyone, anybody	everyone, everybody	no one, nobody	someone, somebody
Places	anywhere	everywhere	nowhere	somewhere
Things	anything	everything	nothing	something

Complete each sentence with an indefinite pronoun.

1. This weekend was boring. I did ___nothing___ .
2. I called the store, but ___nobody___ answered the phone.
3. Jamal left his notebook ___somewhere___ , but he can't remember where.
4. Pippa had an upset stomach, so she didn't eat ___anything___ for lunch.
5. With a flat tire, my dad's car was going ___nowhere___ .

page 16

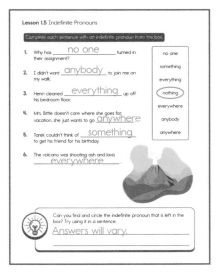

Lesson 1.5 Indefinite Pronouns

Complete each sentence with an indefinite pronoun from the box.

1. Why has ___no one___ turned in their assignment?
2. I didn't want ___anybody___ to join me on my walk.
3. Henri cleaned ___everything___ up off his bedroom floor.
4. Mrs. Bittle doesn't care where she goes for vacation, she just wants to go ___anywhere___ .
5. Tarek couldn't think of ___something___ to get his friend for his birthday.
6. The volcano was shooting ash and lava ___everywhere___ .

no one
something
everything
(nothing)
everywhere
anybody
anywhere

Can you find and circle the indefinite pronoun that is left in the box? Try using it in a sentence.
___Answers will vary.___

page 17

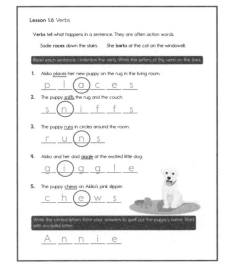

Lesson 1.6 Verbs

Verbs tell what happens in a sentence. They are often action words.

Sadie **races** down the stairs.   She **barks** at the cat on the windowsill.

Read each sentence. Underline the verb. Write the letters of the verb on the lines.

1. Akiko places her new puppy on the rug in the living room.
   p l (a) c e s
2. The puppy sniffs the rug and the couch.
   s (n) i f f s
3. The puppy runs in circles around the room.
   r u (n) s
4. Akiko and her dad giggle at the excited little dog.
   g (i) g g l e
5. The puppy chews on Akiko's pink slipper.
   c h (e) w s

Write the circled letters from your answers to spell out the puppy's name. Start with a capital letter.

A n n i e

page 18

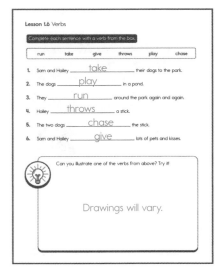

Lesson 1.6 Verbs

Complete each sentence with a verb from the box.

| run | take | give | throws | play | chase |

1. Sam and Hailey ___take___ their dogs to the park.
2. The dogs ___play___ in a pond.
3. They ___run___ around the park again and again.
4. Hailey ___throws___ a stick.
5. The two dogs ___chase___ the stick.
6. Sam and Hailey ___give___ lots of pets and kisses.

Can you illustrate one of the verbs from above? Try it!

Drawings will vary.

page 19

Answer Key

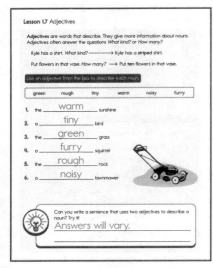

Lesson 1.7 Adjectives

Adjectives are words that describe. They give more information about nouns. Adjectives often answer the questions *What kind?* or *How many?*

Kyle has a shirt. *What kind?* ──→ Kyle has a **striped** shirt.

Put flowers in that vase. *How many?* ──→ Put **ten** flowers in that vase.

Use an adjective from the box to describe each noun.

green	rough	tiny	warm	noisy	furry

1. the __warm__ sunshine
2. a __tiny__ bird
3. the __green__ grass
4. a __furry__ squirrel
5. the __rough__ rock
6. a __noisy__ lawnmower

Can you write a sentence that uses two adjectives to describe a noun? Try it!
__Answers will vary.__

page 20

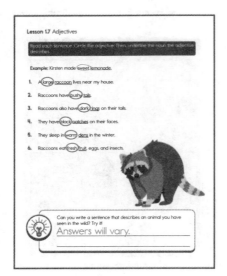

Lesson 1.7 Adjectives

Read each sentence. Circle the adjective. Then, underline the noun the adjective describes.

Example: Kirsten made (sweet) lemonade.

1. A (large) raccoon lives near my house.
2. Raccoons have (bushy) tails.
3. Raccoons also have (dark) rings on their tails.
4. They have (black) patches on their faces.
5. They sleep in (warm) dens in the winter.
6. Raccoons eat (fresh) fruit, eggs, and insects.

Can you write a sentence that describes an animal you have seen in the wild? Try it!
__Answers will vary.__

page 21

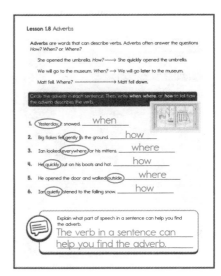

Lesson 1.8 Adverbs

Adverbs are words that can describe verbs. Adverbs often answer the questions *How? When?* or *Where?*

She opened the umbrella. *How?* ──→ She **quickly** opened the umbrella.

We will go to the museum. *When?* ──→ We will go **later** to the museum.

Matt fell. *Where?* ──→ Matt fell **down**.

Circle the adverbs in each sentence. Then, write **when**, **where**, or **how** to tell how the adverb describes the verbs.

1. (Yesterday,) it snowed. __when__
2. Big flakes fell (gently) to the ground. __how__
3. Ian looked (everywhere) for his mittens. __where__
4. He (quickly) put on his boots and hat. __how__
5. He opened the door and walked (outside). __where__
6. Ian (quietly) listened to the falling snow. __how__

Explain what part of speech in a sentence can help you find the adverb.
__The verb in a sentence can help you find the adverb.__

page 22

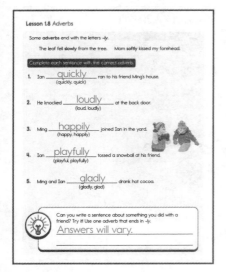

Lesson 1.8 Adverbs

Some adverbs end with the letters -ly.

The leaf fell **slowly** from the tree. Mom **softly** kissed my forehead.

Complete each sentence with the correct adverb.

1. Ian __quickly__ ran to his friend Ming's house.
   (quickly, quick)
2. He knocked __loudly__ at the back door.
   (loud, loudly)
3. Ming __happily__ joined Ian in the yard.
   (happy, happily)
4. Ian __playfully__ tossed a snowball at his friend.
   (playful, playfully)
5. Ming and Ian __gladly__ drank hot cocoa.
   (gladly, glad)

Can you write a sentence about something you did with a friend? Try it! Use one adverb that ends in -ly.
__Answers will vary.__

page 23

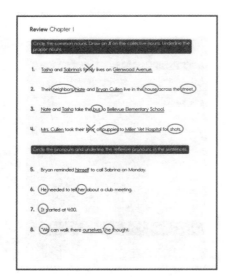

Review Chapter 1

Circle the common nouns. Draw an X on the collective nouns. Underline the proper nouns.

1. <u>Tasha</u> and <u>Sabrina's</u> ✗family lives on <u>Glenwood Avenue</u>.
2. Their (neighbors,) <u>Nate</u> and <u>Bryan Cullen</u> live in the (house) across the (street.)
3. <u>Nate</u> and <u>Tasha</u> take the (bus) to <u>Bellevue Elementary School</u>.
4. <u>Mrs. Cullen</u> took their (litter) of (puppies) to <u>Miller Vet Hospital</u> for (shots.)

Circle the pronouns and underline the reflexive pronouns in the sentences.

5. Bryan reminded <u>himself</u> to call Sabrina on Monday.
6. (He) needed to tell (her) about a club meeting.
7. (It) started at 4:00.
8. (We) can walk there <u>ourselves</u>, (he) thought.

page 24

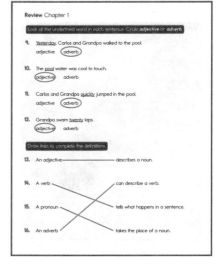

Review Chapter 1

Look at the underlined word in each sentence. Circle **adjective** or **adverb**.

9. <u>Yesterday</u>, Carlos and Grandpa walked to the pool.
   adjective   (adverb)
10. The <u>pool</u> water was cool to touch.
    (adjective)   adverb
11. Carlos and Grandpa <u>quickly</u> jumped in the pool.
    adjective   (adverb)
12. Grandpa swam <u>twenty</u> laps.
    (adjective)   adverb

Draw lines to complete the definitions.

13. An adjective ───── describes a noun.
14. A verb ╲ can describe a verb.
15. A pronoun ╳ tells what happens in a sentence.
16. An adverb ╱ takes the place of a noun.

page 25

Answer Key

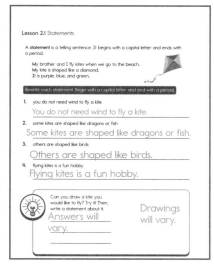

page 28

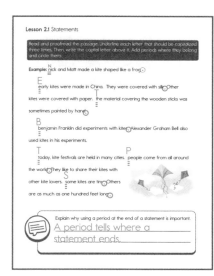

page 29

page 30

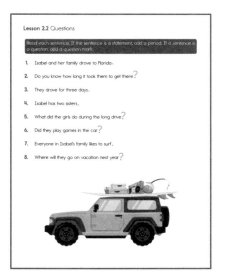

page 31

page 32

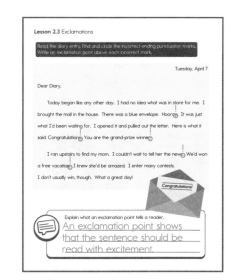

page 33

Answer Key

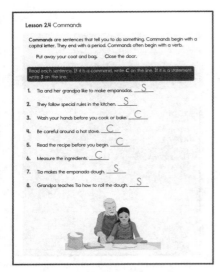

Lesson 2.4 Commands

Commands are sentences that tell you to do something. Commands begin with a capital letter. They end with a period. Commands often begin with a verb.

Put away your coat and bag.   Close the door.

Read each sentence. If it is a command, write **C** on the line. If it is a statement, write **S** on the line.

1. Tia and her grandpa like to make empanadas. __S__
2. They follow special rules in the kitchen. __S__
3. Wash your hands before you cook or bake. __C__
4. Be careful around a hot stove. __C__
5. Read the recipe before you begin. __C__
6. Measure the ingredients. __C__
7. Tia makes the empanada dough. __S__
8. Grandpa teaches Tia how to roll the dough. __S__

page 34

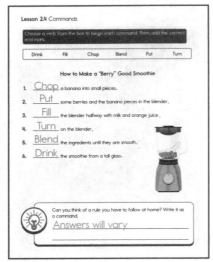

Lesson 2.4 Commands

Choose a verb from the box to begin each command. Then, add the correct end mark.

| Drink | Fill | Chop | Blend | Put | Turn |

How to Make a "Berry" Good Smoothie

1. __Chop__ a banana into small pieces.
2. __Put__ some berries and the banana pieces in the blender.
3. __Fill__ the blender halfway with milk and orange juice.
4. __Turn__ on the blender.
5. __Blend__ the ingredients until they are smooth.
6. __Drink__ the smoothie from a tall glass.

Can you think of a rule you have to follow at home? Write it as a command.
__Answers will vary__

page 35

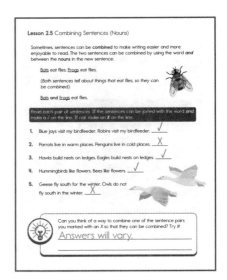

Lesson 2.5 Combining Sentences (Nouns)

Sometimes, sentences can be **combined** to make writing easier and more enjoyable to read. The two sentences can be combined by using the word **and** between the **nouns** in the new sentence.

Bats eat flies. Frogs eat flies.

(Both sentences tell about things that eat flies, so they can be combined.)

Bats and frogs eat flies.

Read each pair of sentences. If the sentences can be joined with the word **and**, make a ✓ on the line. If not, make an ✗ on the line.

1. Blue jays visit my birdfeeder. Robins visit my birdfeeder. __✓__
2. Parrots live in warm places. Penguins live in cold places. __✗__
3. Hawks build nests on ledges. Eagles build nests on ledges. __✓__
4. Hummingbirds like flowers. Bees like flowers. __✓__
5. Geese fly south for the winter. Owls do not fly south in the winter. __✗__

Can you think of a way to combine one of the sentence pairs you marked with an X so that they can be combined? Try it!
__Answers will vary.__

page 36

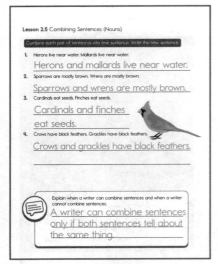

Lesson 2.5 Combining Sentences (Nouns)

Combine each pair of sentences into one sentence. Write the new sentence.

1. Herons live near water. Mallards live near water.
   __Herons and mallards live near water.__
2. Sparrows are mostly brown. Wrens are mostly brown.
   __Sparrows and wrens are mostly brown.__
3. Cardinals eat seeds. Finches eat seeds.
   __Cardinals and finches eat seeds.__
4. Crows have black feathers. Grackles have black feathers.
   __Crows and grackles have black feathers.__

Explain when a writer can combine sentences and when a writer cannot combine sentences.
__A writer can combine sentences only if both sentences tell about the same thing.__

page 37

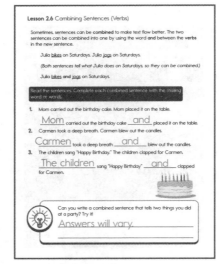

Lesson 2.6 Combining Sentences (Verbs)

Sometimes, sentences can be **combined** to make text flow better. The two sentences can be combined into one by using the word **and** between the **verbs** in the new sentence.

Julia bikes on Saturdays. Julia jogs on Saturdays.

(Both sentences tell what Julia does on Saturdays, so they can be combined.)

Julia bikes and jogs on Saturdays.

Read the sentences. Complete each combined sentence with the missing word or words.

1. Mom carried out the birthday cake. Mom placed it on the table.
   __Mom__ carried out the birthday cake __and__ placed it on the table.
2. Carmen took a deep breath. Carmen blew out the candles.
   __Carmen__ took a deep breath __and__ blew out the candles.
3. The children sang "Happy Birthday." The children clapped for Carmen.
   __The children__ sang "Happy Birthday" __and__ clapped for Carmen.

Can you write a combined sentence that tells two things you did at a party? Try it!
__Answers will vary.__

page 38

Lesson 2.6 Combining Sentences (Verbs)

Combine each pair of sentences into one sentence.

1. Carmen unwrapped her presents. Carmen opened the boxes.
   __Carmen unwrapped her presents and opened the boxes.__
2. Carmen smiled. Carmen thanked her friends for the gifts.
   __Carmen smiled and thanked her friends for the gifts.__
3. Everyone played freeze tag. Everyone had a good time.
   __Everyone played freeze tag and had a good time.__
4. The guests ate cake. The guests drank pink lemonade.
   __The guests ate cake and drank pink lemonade.__

page 39

Answer Key

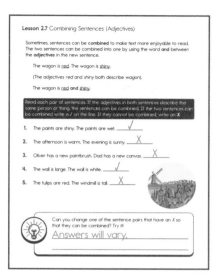

Lesson 2.7 Combining Sentences (Adjectives)

Sometimes, sentences can be **combined** to make text more enjoyable to read. The two sentences can be combined into one by using the word **and** between the **adjectives** in the new sentence.

The wagon is red. The wagon is shiny.

(The adjectives red and shiny both describe wagon).

The wagon is red and shiny.

Read each pair of sentences. If the adjectives in both sentences describe the same person or thing, the sentences can be combined. If the two sentences can be combined write a ✓ on the line. If they cannot be combined, write an **X**.

1. The paints are shiny. The paints are wet. ✓
2. The afternoon is warm. The evening is sunny. X
3. Oliver has a new paintbrush. Dad has a new canvas. X
4. The wall is large. The wall is white. ✓
5. The tulips are red. The windmill is tall. X

Can you change one of the sentence pairs that have an X so that they can be combined? Try it!
Answers will vary.

page 40

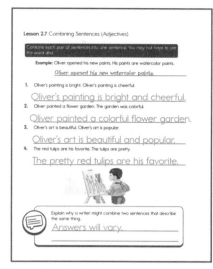

Lesson 2.7 Combining Sentences (Adjectives)

Combine each pair of sentences into one sentence. You may not have to use the word and.

Example: Oliver opened his new paints. His paints are watercolor paints.
Oliver opened his new watercolor paints.

1. Oliver's painting is bright. Oliver's painting is cheerful.
Oliver's painting is bright and cheerful.
2. Oliver painted a flower garden. The garden was colorful.
Oliver painted a colorful flower garden.
3. Oliver's art is beautiful. Oliver's art is popular.
Oliver's art is beautiful and popular.
4. The red tulips are his favorite. The tulips are pretty.
The pretty red tulips are his favorite.

Explain why a writer might combine two sentences that describe the same thing.
Answers will vary.

page 41

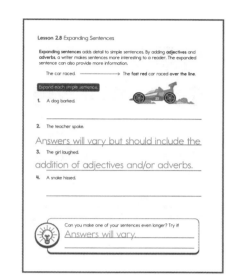

Lesson 2.8 Expanding Sentences

Expanding sentences adds detail to simple sentences. By adding **adjectives** and **adverbs**, a writer makes sentences more interesting to a reader. The expanded sentence can also provide more information.

The car raced. ——————→ The **fast red** car raced **over the line**.

Expand each simple sentence.

1. A dog barked.

2. The teacher spoke.
Answers will vary but should include the
3. The girl laughed.
addition of adjectives and/or adverbs.
4. A snake hissed.

Can you make one of your sentences even longer? Try it!
Answers will vary.

page 42

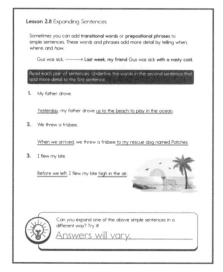

Lesson 2.8 Expanding Sentences

Sometimes you can add **transitional words** or **prepositional phrases** to simple sentences. These words and phrases add more detail by telling when, where, and how.

Gus was sick. ——————→ Last week, my friend Gus was sick with a nasty cold.

Read each pair of sentences. Underline the words in the second sentence that add more detail to the first sentence.

1. My father drove.
Yesterday, my father drove us to the beach to play in the ocean.
2. We threw a frisbee.
When we arrived, we threw a frisbee to my rescue dog named Patches.
3. I flew my kite.
Before we left, I flew my kite high in the air.

Can you expand one of the above simple sentences in a different way? Try it!
Answers will vary.

page 43

Review Chapter 2

Decide if each sentence is a statement (**S**), question (**Q**), exclamation (**E**), or command (**C**). Circle the letter. Then, rewrite each sentence using correct capitalization and ending punctuation.

1. take the trash to the curb — S Q E **C**
Take the trash to the curb.
2. what time do you need to wake up — S **Q** E C
What time do you need to wake up?
3. nat got a new wheel for her hamster — **S** Q E C
Nat got a new wheel for her hamster.
4. that saxophone player is amazing — S Q **E** C
That saxophone player is amazing!
5. can we have pasta for dinner tonight — S **Q** E C
Can we have pasta for dinner tonight?
6. this was the best day ever — S Q **E** C
This was the best day ever!
7. get the ladder from the garage — S Q E **C**
Get the ladder from the garage.
8. matt drives a large white truck — **S** Q E C
Matt drives a large white truck.

page 44

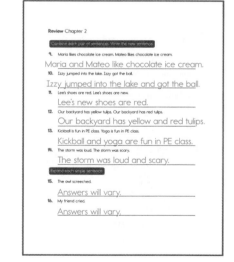

Review Chapter 2

Combine each pair of sentences. Write the new sentence.

9. Maria likes chocolate ice cream. Mateo likes chocolate ice cream.
Maria and Mateo like chocolate ice cream.
10. Izzy jumped into the lake. Izzy got the ball.
Izzy jumped into the lake and got the ball.
11. Lee's shoes are red. Lee's shoes are new.
Lee's new shoes are red.
12. Our backyard has yellow tulips. Our backyard has red tulips.
Our backyard has yellow and red tulips.
13. Kickball is fun in PE class. Yoga is fun in PE class.
Kickball and yoga are fun in PE class.
14. The storm was loud. The storm was scary.
The storm was loud and scary.

Expand each simple sentence.

15. The owl screeched.
Answers will vary.
16. My friend cried.
Answers will vary.

page 45

Answer Key

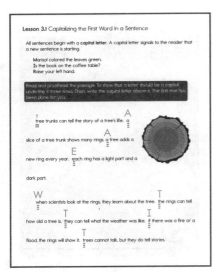

Lesson 3.1 Capitalizing the First Word in a Sentence

All sentences begin with a **capital letter**. A capital letter signals to the reader that a new sentence is starting.

Marisol colored the leaves green.
Is the book on the coffee table?
Raise your left hand.

Read and proofread the passage. To show that a letter should be a capital, underline it three times. Then, write the capital letter above it. The first one has been done for you.

Tree trunks can tell the story of a tree's life. **A** a slice of a tree trunk shows many rings. **A** a tree adds a new ring every year. **E** each ring has a light part and a dark part.

When scientists look at the rings, they learn about the tree. **T**he rings can tell **T**how old a tree is. **T**hey can tell what the weather was like. **I**if there was a fire or a flood, the rings will show it. **T**trees cannot talk, but they do tell stories.

page 48

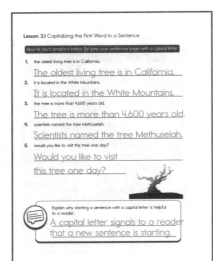

Lesson 3.1 Capitalizing the First Word in a Sentence

Rewrite each sentence below. Be sure your sentences begin with a capital letter.

1. the oldest living tree is in California.
   The oldest living tree is in California.

2. it is located in the White Mountains.
   It is located in the White Mountains.

3. the tree is more than 4,600 years old.
   The tree is more than 4,600 years old.

4. scientists named the tree Methuselah.
   Scientists named the tree Methuselah.

5. would you like to visit this tree one day?
   Would you like to visit this tree one day?

Explain why starting a sentence with a capital letter is helpful to a reader.
A capital letter signals to a reader that a new sentence is starting.

page 49

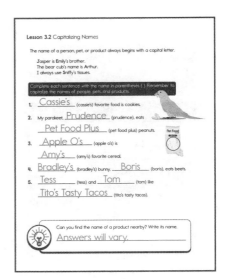

Lesson 3.2 Capitalizing Names

The name of a person, pet, or product always begins with a capital letter.

Jasper is Emily's brother.
The bear cub's name is Arthur.
I always use Sniffy's tissues.

Complete each sentence with the name in parentheses ( ). Remember to capitalize the names of people, pets, and products.

1. Cassie's (cassie's) favorite food is cookies.

2. My parakeet, Prudence (prudence), eats Pet Food Plus (pet food plus) peanuts.

3. Apple O's (apple o's) is Amy's (amy's) favorite cereal.

4. Bradley's (bradley's) bunny, Boris (boris), eats beets.

5. Tess (tess) and Tom (tom) like Tito's Tasty Tacos (tito's tasty tacos).

Can you find the name of a product nearby? Write its name.
Answers will vary.

page 50

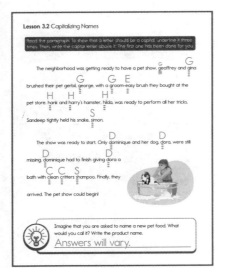

Lesson 3.2 Capitalizing Names

Read the paragraph. To show that a letter should be a capital, underline it three times. Then, write the capital letter above it. The first one has been done for you.

The neighborhood was getting ready to have a pet show. **G**eoffrey and **G**ina **G**brushed their pet gerbil, **G**eorge, with a groom-easy brush they bought at the pet store. **h**ank and **h**arry's hamster, **h**ilda, was ready to perform all her tricks. **S**andeep tightly held his snake, **s**imon.

The show was ready to start. Only **D**ominique and her dog, **D**ora, were still missing. **d**ominique had to finish giving **d**ora a bath with **c**lean **c**ritters **s**hampoo. Finally, they arrived. The pet show could begin!

Imagine that you are asked to name a new pet food. What would you call it? Write the product name.
Answers will vary.

page 51

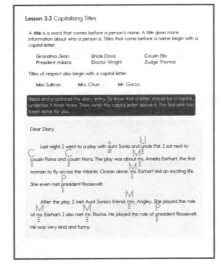

Lesson 3.3 Capitalizing Titles

A **title** is a word that comes before a person's name. A title gives more information about who a person is. Titles that come before a name begin with a capital letter.

Grandma Jean   Uncle Davis   Cousin Ella
President Adams   Doctor Wright   Judge Thomas

Titles of respect also begin with a capital letter.

Miss Sullivan   Mrs. Chun   Mr. Garza

Read and proofread the diary entry. To show that a letter should be a capital, underline it three times. Then, write the capital letter above it. The first one has been done for you.

Dear Diary,

Last night, I went to a play with **A**aunt Sonia and **U**uncle Pat. I sat next to **C**cousin Fiona and **C**cousin Nora. The play was about **M**ms. Amelia Earhart, the first woman to fly across the Atlantic Ocean alone. **M**ms. Earhart led an exciting life. She even met **P**president Roosevelt.

After the play, I met Aunt Sonia's friend, **M**mrs. Angley. She played the role of **M**ms. Earhart. I also met **M**mr. Roche. He played the role of **P**president Roosevelt. He was very kind and funny.

page 52

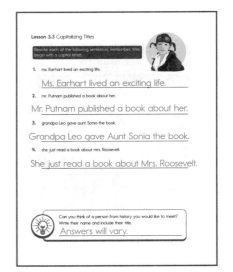

Lesson 3.3 Capitalizing Titles

Rewrite each of the following sentences. Remember, titles begin with a capital letter.

1. ms. Earhart lived an exciting life.
   Ms. Earhart lived an exciting life.

2. mr. Putnam published a book about her.
   Mr. Putnam published a book about her.

3. grandpa Leo gave aunt Sonia the book.
   Grandpa Leo gave Aunt Sonia the book.

4. she just read a book about mrs. Roosevelt.
   She just read a book about Mrs. Roosevelt.

Can you think of a person from history you would like to meet? Write their name and include their title.
Answers will vary.

page 53

Answer Key

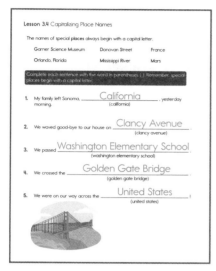

Lesson 3.4 Capitalizing Place Names

The names of special places always begin with a capital letter.

Garner Science Museum   Donovan Street   France
Orlando, Florida   Mississippi River   Mars

Complete each sentence with the word in parentheses ( ). Remember, special places begin with a capital letter.

1. My family left Sonoma, ___California___, yesterday morning.
   (california)

2. We waved good-bye to our house on ___Clancy Avenue___
   (clancy avenue)

3. We passed ___Washington Elementary School___
   (washington elementary school)

4. We crossed the ___Golden Gate Bridge___
   (golden gate bridge)

5. We were on our way across the ___United States___!
   (united states)

page 54

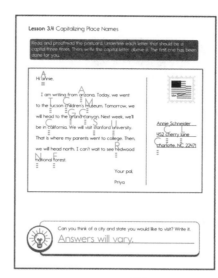

Lesson 3.4 Capitalizing Place Names

Read and proofread the postcard. Underline each letter that should be a capital three times. Then, write the capital letter above it. The first one has been done for you.

Hi annie,

I am writing from arizona. Today, we went to the tucson children's museum. Tomorrow, we will head to the grand canyon. Next week, we'll be in california. We will visit stanford university. That is where my parents went to college. Then, we will head north. I can't wait to see redwood national forest.

Your pal,

Priya

Annie Schneider
452 cherry lane
charlotte, NC 22471

Can you think of a city and state you would like to visit? Write it. ___Answers will vary.___

page 55

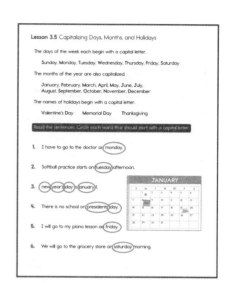

Lesson 3.5 Capitalizing Days, Months, and Holidays

The days of the week each begin with a capital letter.

Sunday, Monday, Tuesday, Wednesday, Thursday, Friday, Saturday

The months of the year are also capitalized.

January, February, March, April, May, June, July, August, September, October, November, December

The names of holidays begin with a capital letter.

Valentine's Day   Memorial Day   Thanksgiving

Read the sentences. Circle each word that should start with a capital letter.

1. I have to go to the doctor on (monday.)

2. Softball practice starts on (tuesday) afternoon.

3. (new) (year's) (day) is (january) 1.

4. There is no school on (presidents') (day.)

5. I will go to my piano lesson on (friday.)

6. We will go to the grocery store on (saturday) morning.

page 56

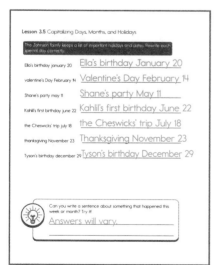

Lesson 3.5 Capitalizing Days, Months, and Holidays

The Johnson family keeps a list of important holidays and dates. Rewrite each special day correctly.

Ella's birthday january 20   ___Ella's birthday January 20___

valentine's Day February 14   ___Valentine's Day February 14___

Shane's party may 11   ___Shane's party May 11___

Kahlil's first birthday june 22   ___Kahlil's first birthday June 22___

the Cheswicks' trip july 18   ___the Cheswicks' trip July 18___

thanksgiving November 23   ___Thanksgiving November 23___

Tyson's birthday december 29   ___Tyson's birthday December 29___

Can you write a sentence about something that happened this week or month? Try it! ___Answers will vary.___

page 57

Review Chapter 3

Rewrite the following sentences with capital letters where they are needed.

1. president kennedy liked animals.
   ___President Kennedy liked animals.___

2. charlie and pushinka were two of his dogs.
   ___Charlie and Pushinka were two of his dogs.___

3. his daughter, caroline, had a pony named macaroni.
   ___His daughter, Caroline, had a pony named Macaroni.___

4. mrs. jackie kennedy had a horse named sardar.
   Mrs. ___Jackie Kennedy had a horse named Sardar.___

Read the paragraph. Write the words that should be capitalized on the lines.

President coolidge had many pets. some pets were ordinary pets. For example, he had a dog named blackberry and a canary named snowflake. others were more unusual. he also had a raccoon named horace. president Coolidge even had a donkey named ebenezer. mrs. Coolidge must have liked animals too!

5. ___Coolidge___ 6. ___Some___ 7. ___Blackberry___

8. ___Snowflake___ 9. ___Others___ 10. ___He___

11. ___Horace___ 12. ___President___ 13. ___Ebenezer___ 14. ___Mrs.___

page 58

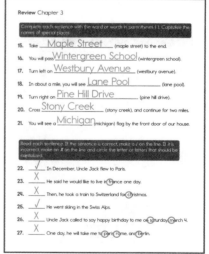

Review Chapter 3

Complete each sentence with the word or words in parentheses ( ). Capitalize the names of special places.

15. Take ___Maple Street___ (maple street) to the end.

16. You will pass ___Wintergreen School___ (wintergreen school).

17. Turn left on ___Westbury Avenue___ (westbury avenue).

18. In about a mile, you will see ___Lane Pool___ (lane pool).

19. Turn right on ___Pine Hill Drive___ (pine hill drive).

20. Cross ___Stony Creek___ (stony creek), and continue for two miles.

21. You will see a ___Michigan___ (michigan) flag by the front door of our house.

Read each sentence. If the sentence is correct, make a ✓ on the line. If it is incorrect, make an X on the line and circle the letter or letters that should be capitalized.

22. ___✓___ In December, Uncle Jack flew to Paris.

23. ___X___ He said he would like to live in (f)rance one day.

24. ___X___ Then, he took a train to Switzerland for (c)hristmas.

25. ___✓___ He went skiing in the Swiss Alps.

26. ___X___ Uncle Jack called to say happy birthday to me on (s)aturday, (m)arch 4.

27. ___X___ One day, he will take me to (p)aris, (r)ome, and (b)erlin.

page 59

Answer Key

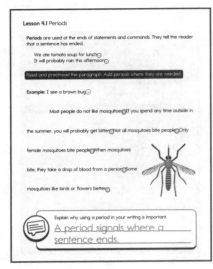

Lesson 4.1 Periods

Periods are used at the ends of statements and commands. They tell the reader that a sentence has ended.

We ate tomato soup for lunch.
It will probably rain this afternoon.

Read and proofread the paragraph. Add periods where they are needed.

Example: I see a brown bug.

Most people do not like mosquitoes. If you spend any time outside in the summer, you will probably get bitten. Not all mosquitoes bite people. Only female mosquitoes bite people. When mosquitoes bite, they take a drop of blood from a person. Some mosquitoes like birds or flowers better.

Explain why using a period in your writing is important.
A period signals where a sentence ends.

page 62

Lesson 4.1 Periods

Read the sentences. Add a period to the end of each statement.

1. There are thousands of types of mosquitoes.
2. Mosquitoes like human sweat.
3. Some people never get mosquito bites.
4. Mosquitoes lay eggs in still water.
5. Bug spray can protect you from bites.

Imagine you are about to hike a rainforest trail that has many mosquitoes. There is a sign at the beginning telling you what to do to protect yourself. Draw the sign. Include at least five commands you might read on the sign.

Drawings will vary.

page 63

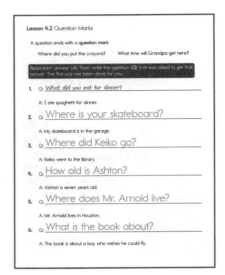

Lesson 4.2 Question Marks

A question ends with a **question mark**.

Where did you put the crayons?   What time will Grandpa get here?

Read each answer (A). Then, write the question (Q) that was asked to get that answer. The first one has been done for you.

1. Q: What did you eat for dinner?
   A: I ate spaghetti for dinner.
2. Q: Where is your skateboard?
   A: My skateboard is in the garage.
3. Q: Where did Keiko go?
   A: Keiko went to the library.
4. Q: How old is Ashton?
   A: Ashton is seven years old.
5. Q: Where does Mr. Arnold live?
   A: Mr. Arnold lives in Houston.
6. Q: What is the book about?
   A: The book is about a boy who wishes he could fly.

page 64

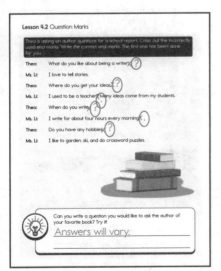

Lesson 4.2 Question Marks

Theo is asking an author questions for a school report. Cross out the incorrectly used end marks. Write the correct end marks. The first one has been done for you.

Theo: What do you like about being a writer?
Ms. Li: I love to tell stories.
Theo: Where do you get your ideas?
Ms. Li: I used to be a teacher. Many ideas come from my students.
Theo: When do you write?
Ms. Li: I write for about four hours every morning.
Theo: Do you have any hobbies?
Ms. Li: I like to garden, ski, and do crossword puzzles.

Can you write a question you would like to ask the author of your favorite book? Try it!
Answers will vary.

page 65

Lesson 4.3 Exclamation Points

An **exclamation point** is used to end a sentence that is exciting. Sometimes exclamation points are used to show surprise.

Look at the rainbow!   I loved that movie!   Wow!

Read the poster. Add the missing end marks where they are needed.

Hooray!

The Bellview Fair
is coming to town in July!

Win great prizes!

Ride the biggest Ferris wheel in Clark County!

Sample tasty foods!

Admission is $3.00 for adults and $2.00 for kids under twelve.

The fair opens July 6 and closes July 12.
Don't miss all the fun!

page 66

Lesson 4.3 Exclamation Points

Read each pair of sentences. One sentence should end with a period. The other should end with an exclamation point. Add the correct end marks.

1. I went to the Bellview Fair.
   I had the best time!
2. I played a game called Toss the Ring.
   I won four stuffed animals!
3. All the sheep escaped from their pen!
   It did not take the farmers long to catch them, though.
4. I ate a snow cone and some cotton candy.
   The cotton candy got stuck in my hair!

Can you write an exclamation about an exciting place you've been? Try it!
Answers will vary.

page 67

Answer Key

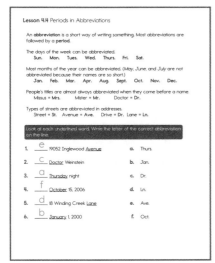

page 68

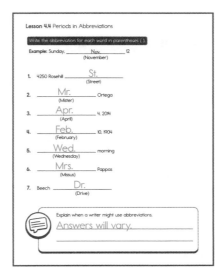

page 69

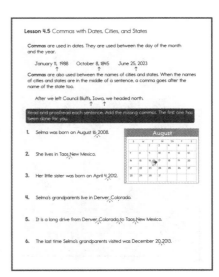

page 70

page 71

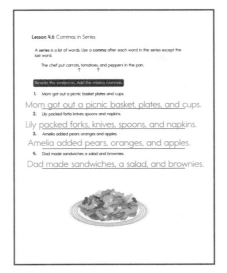

page 72

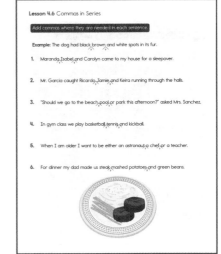

page 73

Answer Key

Lesson 4.7 Commas in Letters

In a letter, a **comma** follows the greeting and the closing.

Dear Mr. Wong,   Your friend,   Sincerely,

Circle the commas in the letter.

August 2, 2023

Dear Helga,

It is hot and sunny here today. I am going to the park nearby to play in the splash pad with a few friends. Do you like to play in water?

What is the weather like in Iceland this time of year? Please write back!

Your pen pal,

Amelia

Can you write the greeting and closing for a letter you would write to a friend? Try it!
Answers will vary.

page 74

Lesson 4.7 Commas in Letters

Read the letter. Add the missing commas where they are needed. The first one has been done for you.

June 19, 2022

Dear Grandma,

Yesterday, we went to the park. Lily, Amelia, and Mom shook out the picnic blanket. Dad carried the basket, the drinks, and the toys from the car. We all ate some salad, a sandwich, and a fruit.

Deepak, Sita, and Raj were at the park with their parents too. We played tag and fed the ducks. Later, we shared our brownies with the Nair family. I wish you could have been there!

Love,

Max

page 75

Lesson 4.8 Commas in Compound Sentences

A **compound sentence** is made up of two smaller sentences. The smaller sentences are joined by a comma and often the word *and* or *but*.

Michelle went to the store. She bought some markers.
Michelle went to the store, and she bought some markers.

Bats sleep during the day. They are active at night.
Bats sleep during the day, but they are active at night.

Combine each pair of sentences by using a comma and the word *and* or *but*.

1. Abby rode her bike. Gilbert rode his scooter.
   Abby rode her bike, and Gilbert rode his scooter.

2. My new bedroom is big. My old bedroom was bigger.
   My new bedroom is big, but my old bedroom was bigger.

3. The black cat is beautiful. The orange cat is friendly.
   The black cat is beautiful, and the orange cat is friendly.

4. Roberto is a fast swimmer. Sophie is a faster swimmer.
   Roberto is a fast swimmer, but Sophie is a faster swimmer.

page 76

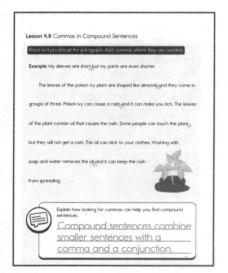

Lesson 4.8 Commas in Compound Sentences

Read and proofread the paragraph. Add commas where they are needed.

Example: My sleeves are short, but my pants are even shorter.

The leaves of the poison ivy plant are shaped like almonds, and they come in groups of three. Poison ivy can cause a rash, and it can make you itch. The leaves of the plant contain oil that causes the rash. Some people can touch the plant, but they will not get a rash. The oil can stick to your clothes. Washing with soap and water removes the oil, and it can keep the rash from spreading.

Explain how looking for commas can help you find compound sentences.
Compound sentences combine smaller sentences with a comma and a conjunction.

page 77

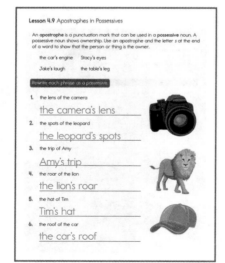

Lesson 4.9 Apostrophes in Possessives

An **apostrophe** is a punctuation mark that can be used in a **possessive** noun. A possessive noun shows ownership. Use an apostrophe and the letter *s* at the end of a word to show that the person or thing is the owner.

the car's engine   Stacy's eyes
Jake's laugh   the table's leg

Rewrite each phrase as a possessive.

1. the lens of the camera
   the camera's lens

2. the spots of the leopard
   the leopard's spots

3. the trip of Amy
   Amy's trip

4. the roar of the lion
   the lion's roar

5. the hat of Tim
   Tim's hat

6. the roof of the car
   the car's roof

page 78

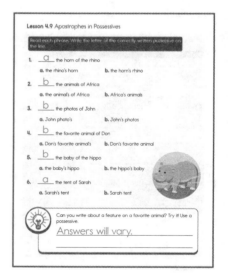

Lesson 4.9 Apostrophes in Possessives

Read each phrase. Write the letter of the correctly written possessive on the line.

1. __a__ the horn of the rhino
   a. the rhino's horn   b. the horn's rhino

2. __b__ the animals of Africa
   a. the animals of Africa   b. Africa's animals

3. __b__ the photos of John
   a. John photo's   b. John's photos

4. __b__ the favorite animal of Don
   a. Don's favorite animal's   b. Don's favorite animal

5. __b__ the baby of the hippo
   a. the baby's hippo   b. the hippo's baby

6. __a__ the tent of Sarah
   a. Sarah's tent   b. Sarah tent

Can you write about a feature on a favorite animal? Try it! Use a possessive.
Answers will vary.

page 79

Answer Key

page 80

Lesson 4.10 Quotation Marks in Dialogue

Quotation marks are used around the exact words a person says. One set of quotation marks is used before the first word the person says. Another set is used at the end of the person's words. The exact words people say are sometimes called **dialogue**. Quotation marks are used to show which words are dialogue.

Jamal said, "I am going to play in a piano recital on Saturday."

"Do you like fresh apple pie?" asked the baker.

"Hooray!" shouted Sydney. "Today is a snow day!"

Remember to put the second pair of quotation marks after the punctuation mark that ends the sentence.

Read each sentence. Underline the speaker's exact words. Then, add a set of quotation marks before and after the speaker's words.

1. "Would you like to go skiing this afternoon?" asked Mom.
2. Alyssa asked, "Where will we go?"
3. Mom said, "Wintergreen Mountain is not too far away."
4. "Can I bring a friend?" asked Zane.
5. Mom said, "You can each bring along one friend."
6. Alyssa said, "Riley will be so excited!"

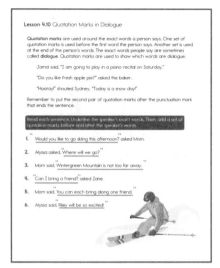

page 81

Lesson 4.10 Quotation Marks in Dialogue

Read each sentence. Write the sentence again. Add quotation marks where they are needed. Remember to find the speaker's exact words first.

1. Have you ever been skiing? Zane asked his friend.

   "Have you ever been skiing?" Zane asked his friend.

2. Joey said, No, but it sounds like fun.

   Joey said, "No, but it sounds like fun."

3. Riley said, My grandpa taught me how to ski.

   Riley said, "My grandpa taught me how to ski."

4. She added, He lives near the mountains in Vermont.

   She added, "He lives near the mountains in Vermont."

page 82

Lesson 4.11 Titles of Books and Movies

The titles of books and movies are underlined in text. This lets the reader know that the underlined words are part of a title.

Cristina's favorite movie is Because of Winn-Dixie.
Harry wrote a book report on Nate the Great and the Musical Note.

Underline the title of each book or movie.

1. Tom Hanks was the voice of Woody in the movie Toy Story.
2. Mara Wilson played Matilda Wormwood in the movie Matilda.
3. In the movie Shrek, Cameron Diaz was the voice of Princess Fiona.
4. The movie Fly Away Home is based on a true story.
5. Harriet the Spy is the name of a book and a movie.

page 83

Lesson 4.11 Titles of Books and Movies

Read the passage. Underline the titles.

Jon Scieszka (say shess-ka) is a popular author. He has written many books for children. He is best known for his book The Stinky Cheese Man and Other Fairly Stupid Tales. Jon has always loved books. Dr. Seuss's famous book Green Eggs and Ham made Jon feel like he could be a writer one day. In 1989, Jon wrote The True Story of the Three Little Pigs. Many children think his books are very funny. They also like the pictures. Lane Smith draws the pictures for many of Jon's books. They worked together on the book Math Curse. Their book Science Verse is also popular.

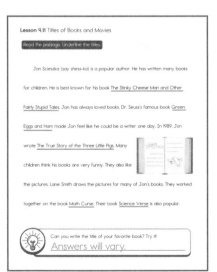

Can you write the title of your favorite book? Try it!
Answers will vary.

page 84

Review Chapter 4

Read each sentence. Add the correct end mark on the line.

1. Thursday started out like any other day .
2. I ate breakfast and went to school .
3. When I came home, my mom and dad told me the news .
4. Do you know what they said ?
5. I am going to be a big brother !

Rewrite each phrase. Use an abbreviation in place of the underlined word.

6. Missus Lahiri Mrs. Lahiri
7. Delmar Lane Delmar Ln.
8. Tuesday, August 2 Tuesday, Aug. 2
9. November 22, 2004 Nov. 22, 2004
10. Doctor White Dr. White

Rewrite each phrase as a possessive.

11. the cat of Enrique Enrique's cat
12. the shirt of Cassie Cassie's shirt

page 85

Review Chapter 4

Read the letter. Add the missing commas.

Dear Quinn,

I need to write a letter for school. I chose to write to you about Peter Jenkins. He was born on July 8, 1951 in Greenwich, Connecticut. Peter is best known for walking across America. He began his walk on October 15, 1973. He walked from Alfred, New York to Florence, Oregon. His walk ended on January 18, 1979.

Today, Peter lives on a farm in Spring Hill, Tennessee. His children are named Rebekah, Jedidiah, Luke, Aaron, Brooke, and Julianne. Peter likes to travel, write, and speak to people about his adventures. I hope you liked learning about Peter. I'll talk to you soon!

Your friend,
Eli

Complete each sentence with your own answer. Use quotation marks to show that someone is speaking. Don't forget to underline titles.

13. _____ is the funniest book I have ever read.
14. I think everyone should see the movie _____
15. When she came from the dentist, Beatriz said, _____
16. Steven looked at his watch and said, _____

Answers will vary.

Answer Key

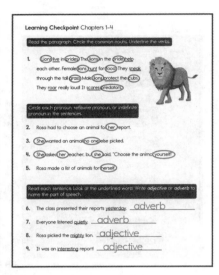

Learning Checkpoint Chapters 1–4

Read the paragraph. Circle the common nouns. Underline the verbs.

1. (Lions) live in (prides.) The (lions) in the (pride) help each other. Female (lions) hunt for (food.) They sneak through the tall (grass.) Male (lions) protect the (cubs.) They roar really loud! It scares (predators.)

Circle each pronoun, reflexive pronoun, or indefinite pronoun in the sentences.

2. Rosa had to choose an animal for (her) report.
3. (She) wanted an animal (no one) else picked.
4. (She) asked (her) teacher, but (she) said, "Choose the animal (yourself.)"
5. Rosa made a list of animals for (herself.)

Read each sentence. Look at the underlined word. Write adjective or adverb to name the part of speech.

6. The class presented their reports yesterday. __adverb__
7. Everyone listened quietly. __adverb__
8. Rosa picked the mighty lion. __adjective__
9. It was an interesting report! __adjective__

page 86

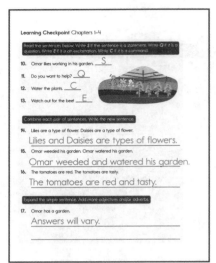

Learning Checkpoint Chapters 1–4

Read the sentences below. Write S if the sentence is a statement. Write Q if it is a question. Write E if it is an exclamation. Write C if it is a command.

10. Omar likes working in his garden. __S__
11. Do you want to help? __Q__
12. Water the plants. __C__
13. Watch out for the bee! __E__

Combine each pair of sentences. Write the new sentence.

14. Lilies are a type of flower. Daisies are a type of flower.
    __Lilies and Daisies are types of flowers.__
15. Omar weeded his garden. Omar watered his garden.
    __Omar weeded and watered his garden.__
16. The tomatoes are red. The tomatoes are tasty.
    __The tomatoes are red and tasty.__

Expand the simple sentence. Add more adjectives and/or adverbs.

17. Omar has a garden.
    __Answers will vary.__

page 87

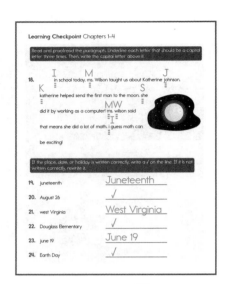

Learning Checkpoint Chapters 1–4

Read and proofread the paragraph. Underline each letter that should be a capital letter three times. Then, write the capital letter above it.

18.   I   M   J
    in school today, ms. Wilson taught us about Katherine johnson.
    K   S
    katherine helped send the first man to the moon. she
                        MW
    did it by working as a computer! ms. wilson said
                T
    that means she did a lot of math. i guess math can
    be exciting!

If the place, date, or holiday is written correctly, write a ✓ on the line. If it is not written correctly, rewrite it.

19. juneteenth   __Juneteenth__
20. August 26   __✓__
21. west Virginia   __West Virginia__
22. Douglass Elementary __✓__
23. june 19   __June 19__
24. Earth Day   __✓__

page 88

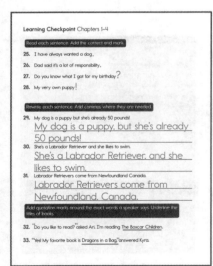

Learning Checkpoint Chapters 1–4

Read each sentence. Add the correct end mark.

25. I have always wanted a dog.
26. Dad said it's a lot of responsibility.
27. Do you know what I got for my birthday?
28. My very own puppy!

Rewrite each sentence. Add commas where they are needed.

29. My dog is a puppy but she's already 50 pounds!
    __My dog is a puppy, but she's already 50 pounds!__
30. She's a Labrador Retriever and she likes to swim.
    __She's a Labrador Retriever, and she likes to swim.__
31. Labrador Retrievers come from Newfoundland Canada.
    __Labrador Retrievers come from Newfoundland, Canada.__

Add quotation marks around the exact words a speaker says. Underline the titles of books.

32. "Do you like to read?" asked Ari. I'm reading The Boxcar Children.
33. "Yes! My favorite book is Dragons in a Bag," answered Kyra.

page 89

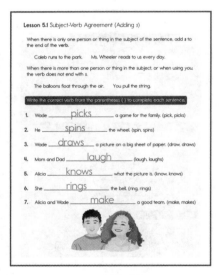

Lesson 5.1 Subject-Verb Agreement (Adding s)

When there is only one person or thing in the subject of the sentence, add s to the end of the verb.

Caleb runs to the park.   Ms. Wheeler reads to us every day.

When there is more than one person or thing in the subject, or when using you, the verb does not end with s.

The balloons float through the air.   You pull the string.

Write the correct verb from the parentheses ( ) to complete each sentence.

1. Wade __picks__ a game for the family. (pick, picks)
2. He __spins__ the wheel. (spin, spins)
3. Wade __draws__ a picture on a big sheet of paper. (draw, draws)
4. Mom and Dad __laugh__ (laugh, laughs)
5. Alicia __knows__ what the picture is. (know, knows)
6. She __rings__ the bell. (ring, rings)
7. Alicia and Wade __make__ a good team. (make, makes)

page 92

Lesson 5.1 Subject-Verb Agreement (Adding s)

Read each sentence. Add an s to the end of the verb if needed.

1. The Andersons love___ game night.
2. Alicia choose__S__ the game.
3. She pick__S__ her favorite board game.
4. Mom, Dad, Alicia, and Wade roll___ the dice.
5. Wade take__S__ the first turn.
6. He move__S__ his piece four spaces.
7. Mom roll__S__ the dice.
8. Uh-oh! Mom lose__S__ her turn.
9. Mom never win__S__ this game!

Can you write two sentences using the verbs play and plays? Try it!
__Answers will vary.__

page 93

Answer Key

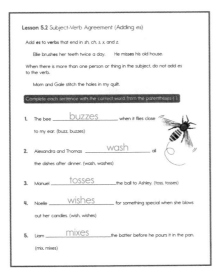

Lesson 5.2 Subject-Verb Agreement (Adding *es*)

Add *es* to verbs that end in *sh, ch, s, x,* and *z.*

Ellie brushes her teeth twice a day.   He misses his old house.

When there is more than one person or thing in the subject, do not add *es* to the verb.

Mom and Gale stitch the holes in my quilt.

Complete each sentence with the correct word from the parentheses ( ).

1. The bee _____**buzzes**_____ when it flies close to my ear. (buzz, buzzes)

2. Alexandra and Thomas _____**wash**_____ all the dishes after dinner. (wash, washes)

3. Manuel _____**tosses**_____ the ball to Ashley. (toss, tosses)

4. Noelle _____**wishes**_____ for something special when she blows out her candles. (wish, wishes)

5. Liam _____**mixes**_____ the batter before he pours it in the pan. (mix, mixes)

page 94

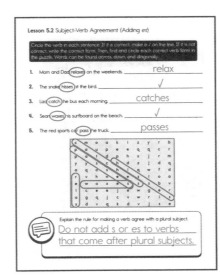

Lesson 5.2 Subject-Verb Agreement (Adding *es*)

Circle the verb in each sentence. If it is correct, make a ✓ on the line. If it is not correct, write the correct form. Then, find and circle each correct verb form in the puzzle. Words can be found across, down, and diagonally.

1. Mom and Dad (relaxes) on the weekends. _____**relax**_____

2. The snake (hisses) at the bird. _____✓_____

3. Liza (catch) the bus each morning. _____**catches**_____

4. Sean (waxes) his surfboard on the beach. _____✓_____

5. The red sports car (pass) the truck. _____**passes**_____

Explain the rule for making a verb agree with a plural subject. **Do not add s or es to verbs that come after plural subjects.**

page 95

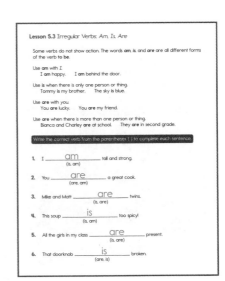

Lesson 5.3 Irregular Verbs: *Am, Is, Are*

Some verbs do not show action. The words **am, is,** and **are** are all different forms of the verb to **be.**

Use **am** with *I.*
    I **am** happy.   I **am** behind the door.

Use **is** when there is only one person or thing.
    Tommy is my brother.   The sky **is** blue.

Use **are** with you.
    You **are** lucky.   You **are** my friend.

Use **are** when there is more than one person or thing.
    Bianca and Charley **are** at school.   They **are** in second grade.

Write the correct verb from the parentheses ( ) to complete each sentence.

1. I _____**am**_____ tall and strong. (is, am)

2. You _____**are**_____ a great cook. (are, am)

3. Mike and Matt _____**are**_____ twins. (is, are)

4. This soup _____**is**_____ too spicy! (is, am)

5. All the girls in my class _____**are**_____ present. (is, are)

6. That doorknob _____**is**_____ broken. (are, is)

page 96

Lesson 5.3 Irregular Verbs: *Am, Is, Are*

Read the diary entry. Cross out each incorrect verb. Then, write the correct verb above it.

Thursday, May 27

Dear Diary,

Victoria ~~are~~ **is** my friend. She knows lots of jokes. Today, I told her, "You ~~am~~ **are** the funniest person I know! I ~~are~~ **am** glad to be your friend."

We ~~is~~ **are** in a club together. Owen and Rachel ~~is~~ **are** in the club, too.

We learn all kinds of jokes. Knock-knock jokes ~~is~~ **are** my favorite.

Riddles ~~am~~ **are** Victoria's favorite.

Owen ~~are~~ **is** older than us. He ~~am~~ **is** in third grade. He tells us all the third-grade jokes. We spend a lot of time laughing!

page 97

Lesson 5.4 Irregular Verbs: *Has, Have*

Some verbs do not show action. The verb to **have** does not show action. **Has** and **have** are different forms of the verb to **have.**

Use **have** with *I* or you.
    I **have** six cats.   You **have** a bird.

Use **have** when there is more than one person or thing.
    We **have** a French lesson this afternoon.   They **have** a green car.
    Maureen and Ramon **have** brown hair.   The tree and plant **have** leaves.

Use **has** when there is only one person or thing.
    She **has** two braids.   Lex **has** a book about fossils.

Complete each sentence with the correct verb form in parentheses ( ).

1. Maple trees and oak trees _____**have**_____ similar leaves. (has, have)

2. A gingko tree _____**has**_____ leaves that look like fans. (has, have)

3. We _____**have**_____ a large fir tree in the backyard. (has, have)

4. The Maddens _____**have**_____ many trees that bloom in the spring. (has, have)

5. Lila _____**has**_____ an enormous, old maple tree in the front yard. (has, have)

page 98

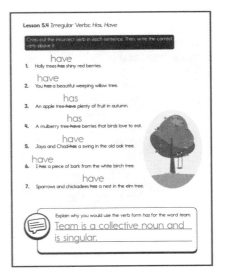

Lesson 5.4 Irregular Verbs: *Has, Have*

Cross out the incorrect verb in each sentence. Then, write the correct verb above it.

1. Holly trees ~~has~~ **have** shiny red berries.

2. You ~~has~~ **have** a beautiful weeping willow tree.

3. An apple tree ~~have~~ **has** plenty of fruit in autumn.

4. A mulberry tree ~~have~~ **has** berries that birds love to eat.

5. Jaya and Chad ~~has~~ **have** a swing in the old oak tree.

6. I ~~has~~ **have** a piece of bark from the white birch tree.

7. Sparrows and chickadees ~~has~~ **have** a nest in the elm tree.

Explain why you would use the verb form has for the word team. **Team is a collective noun and is singular.**

page 99

Answer Key

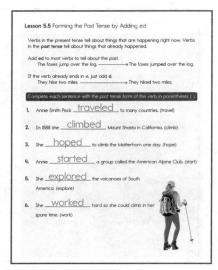

page 100

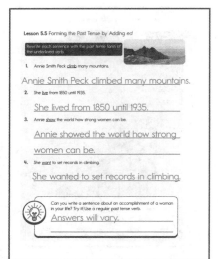

page 101

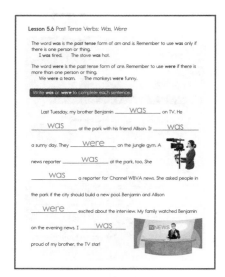

page 102

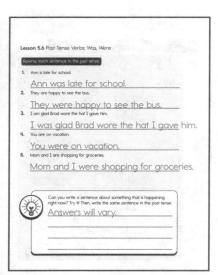

page 103

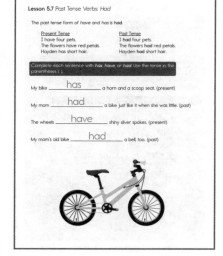

page 104

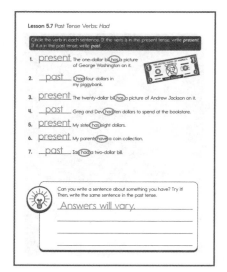

page 105

Answer Key

Lesson 5.8 Past Tense Verbs: *Went*

The past tense form of *go* and *goes* is **went**.

Present Tense
We go to the fair with our cousins.
Lorenzo goes to Florida.

Past Tense
We **went** to the fair with our cousins.
Lorenzo **went** to Florida.

Rewrite each sentence in the past tense.

1. We go to the store.
   We went to the store.
2. We go sledding with Miki and Ted.
   We went sledding with Miki and Ted.
3. Sanjay goes home at noon.
   Sanjay went home at noon.
4. Rae goes to her singing lesson today.
   Rae went to her singing lesson today.

page 106

Lesson 5.8 Past Tense Verbs: *Went*

Read the text. Cross out the verbs that are in the wrong tense. Write the correct verbs above them.

went
When my dad was little, his family ~~goes~~ to a cabin every summer. He loved
went
the little cabin in the woods. His cousins came to visit. Everyone ~~goes~~ swimming in
went
the lake. They ~~go~~ on long bike rides. They built forts in the woods. Grandma and
went
Grandpa ~~go~~ for long walks. Once the entire family came from miles away. They
went
~~go~~ to a big family party on the beach.

Dad loved those summers in the woods.

Some day, he will take us to see the old cabin.

Explain what types of words in a text tell you what verb tense to use.
Words that tell about the past
are clues for what tense to use.

page 107

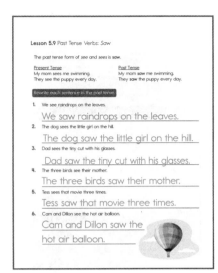

Lesson 5.9 Past Tense Verbs: *Saw*

The past tense form of *see* and *sees* is **saw**.

Present Tense
My mom sees me swimming.
They see the puppy every day.

Past Tense
My mom **saw** me swimming.
They **saw** the puppy every day.

Rewrite each sentence in the past tense.

1. We see raindrops on the leaves.
   We saw raindrops on the leaves.
2. The dog sees the little girl on the hill.
   The dog saw the little girl on the hill.
3. Dad sees the tiny cut with his glasses.
   Dad saw the tiny cut with his glasses.
4. The three birds see their mother.
   The three birds saw their mother.
5. Tess sees that movie three times.
   Tess saw that movie three times.
6. Cam and Dillon see the hot air balloon.
   Cam and Dillon saw the hot air balloon.

page 108

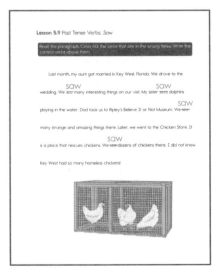

Lesson 5.9 Past Tense Verbs: *Saw*

Read the paragraph. Cross out the verbs that are in the wrong tense. Write the correct verbs above them.

Last month, my aunt got married in Key West, Florida. We drove to the
saw   saw
wedding. We ~~see~~ many interesting things on our visit. My sister ~~sees~~ dolphins
saw
playing in the water. Dad took us to Ripley's Believe It or Not Museum. We ~~see~~
many strange and amazing things there. Later, we went to the Chicken Store. It
saw
is a place that rescues chickens. We ~~see~~ dozens of chickens there. I did not know

Key West had so many homeless chickens!

page 109

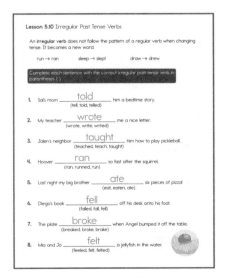

Lesson 5.10 Irregular Past Tense Verbs

An **irregular verb** does not follow the pattern of a regular verb when changing tense. It becomes a new word.

run → ran   sleep → slept   draw → drew

Complete each sentence with the correct irregular past tense verb in parentheses ( ).

1. Sal's mom _____told_____ him a bedtime story.
   (tell, told, telled)
2. My teacher _____wrote_____ me a nice letter.
   (wrote, write, writed)
3. Jalen's neighbor _____taught_____ him how to play pickleball.
   (teached, teach, taught)
4. Hoover _____ran_____ so fast after the squirrel.
   (ran, runned, run)
5. Last night my big brother _____ate_____ six pieces of pizza!
   (eat, eaten, ate)
6. Diego's book _____fell_____ off his desk onto his foot.
   (falled, fall, fell)
7. The plate _____broke_____ when Angel bumped it off the table.
   (breaked, broke, brake)
8. Mia and Jo _____felt_____ a jellyfish in the water.
   (feeled, felt, fetted)

page 110

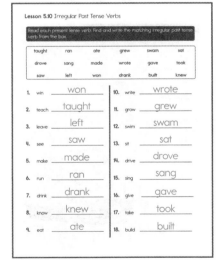

Lesson 5.10 Irregular Past Tense Verbs

Read each present tense verb. Find and write the matching irregular past tense verb from the box.

taught	ran	ate	grew	swam	sat
drove	sang	made	wrote	gave	took
saw	left	won	drank	built	knew

1. win — won
2. teach — taught
3. leave — left
4. see — saw
5. make — made
6. run — ran
7. drink — drank
8. know — knew
9. eat — ate
10. write — wrote
11. grow — grew
12. swim — swam
13. sit — sat
14. drive — drove
15. sing — sang
16. give — gave
17. take — took
18. build — built

page 111

Answer Key

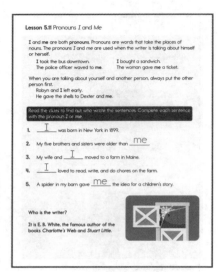

page 112

page 113

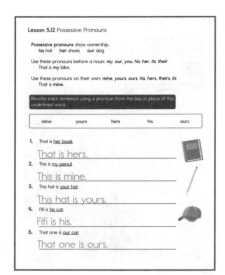

page 114

page 115

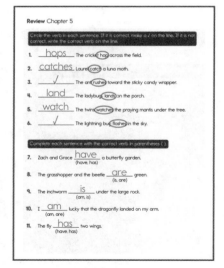

page 116

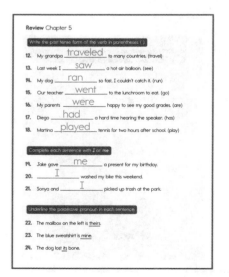

page 117

Answer Key

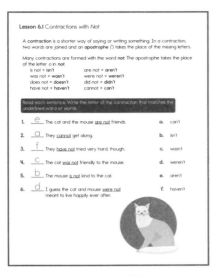

Lesson 6.1 Contractions with *Not*

A **contraction** is a shorter way of saying or writing something. In a contraction, two words are joined and an **apostrophe** (') takes the place of the missing letters.

Many contractions are formed with the word *not*. The apostrophe takes the place of the letter o in *not*.

is not = isn't	are not = aren't
was not = wasn't	were not = weren't
does not = doesn't	did not = didn't
have not = haven't	cannot = can't

Read each sentence. Write the letter of the contraction that matches the underlined word or words.

1. __e__ The cat and the mouse <u>are not</u> friends.   a. can't
2. __a__ They <u>cannot</u> get along.   b. isn't
3. __f__ They <u>have not</u> tried very hard, though.   c. wasn't
4. __c__ The cat <u>was not</u> friendly to the mouse.   d. weren't
5. __b__ The mouse <u>is not</u> kind to the cat.   e. aren't
6. __d__ I guess the cat and mouse <u>were not</u> meant to live happily ever after.   f. haven't

page 120

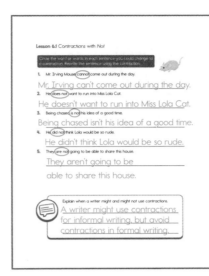

Lesson 6.1 Contractions with *Not*

Circle the word or words in each sentence you could change to a contraction. Rewrite the sentence using the contraction.

1. Mr. Irving Mouse (cannot) come out during the day.
   Mr. Irving can't come out during the day.
2. He (does not) want to run into Miss Lola Cat.
   He doesn't want to run into Miss Lola Cat.
3. Being chased (is not) his idea of a good time.
   Being chased isn't his idea of a good time.
4. He (did not) think Lola would be so rude.
   He didn't think Lola would be so rude.
5. They (are not) going to be able to share this house.
   They aren't going to be
   able to share this house.

Explain when a writer might and might not use contractions.
A writer might use contractions for informal writing, but avoid contractions in formal writing.

page 121

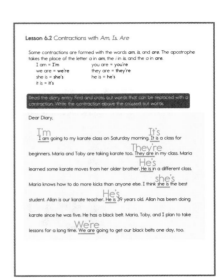

Lesson 6.2 Contractions with *Am, Is, Are*

Some contractions are formed with the words **am**, **is**, and **are**. The apostrophe takes the place of the letter a in **am**, the i in **is**, and the a in **are**.

I am = I'm	you are = you're
we are = we're	they are = they're
she is = she's	he is = he's
it is = it's	

Read the diary entry. Find and cross out words that can be replaced with a contraction. Write the contraction above the crossed out words.

Dear Diary,

      I'm
<u>I am</u> going to my karate class on Saturday morning. ~~It is~~ (It's) a class for
beginners. Maria and Toby are taking karate too. ~~They are~~ (They're) in my class. Maria
learned some karate moves from her older brother. ~~He is~~ (He's) in a different class.
Maria knows how to do more kicks than anyone else. I think ~~she is~~ (she's) the best
student. Allan is our karate teacher. ~~He is~~ (He's) 39 years old. Allan has been doing
karate since he was five. He has a black belt. Maria, Toby, and I plan to take
lessons for a long time. ~~We are~~ (We're) going to get our black belts one day, too.

page 122

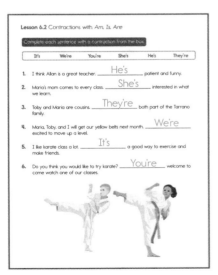

Lesson 6.2 Contractions with *Am, Is, Are*

Complete each sentence with a contraction from the box.

It's	We're	You're	She's	He's	They're

1. I think Allan is a great teacher. __He's__ patient and funny.
2. Maria's mom comes to every class. __She's__ interested in what we learn.
3. Toby and Maria are cousins. __They're__ both part of the Tarrano family.
4. Maria, Toby, and I will get our yellow belts next month. __We're__ excited to move up a level.
5. I like karate class a lot. __It's__ a good way to exercise and make friends.
6. Do you think you would like to try karate? __You're__ welcome to come watch one of our classes.

page 123

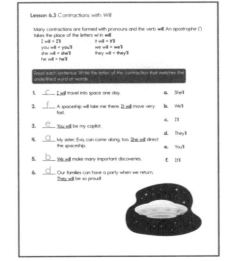

Lesson 6.3 Contractions with *Will*

Many contractions are formed with pronouns and the verb *will*. An apostrophe (') takes the place of the letters wi in *will*.

I will = I'll	it will = it'll
you will = you'll	we will = we'll
she will = she'll	they will = they'll
he will = he'll	

Read each sentence. Write the letter of the contraction that matches the underlined word or words.

1. __c__ <u>I will</u> travel into space one day.   a. She'll
2. __f__ A spaceship will take me there. <u>It will</u> move very fast.   b. We'll
3. __e__ <u>You will</u> be my copilot.   c. I'll
4. __a__ My sister, Eva, can come along, too. <u>She will</u> direct the spaceship.   d. They'll
5. __b__ <u>We will</u> make many important discoveries.   e. You'll
6. __d__ Our families can have a party when we return. <u>They will</u> be so proud!   f. It'll

page 124

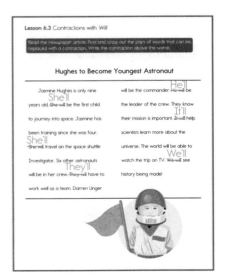

Lesson 6.3 Contractions with *Will*

Read the newspaper article. Find and cross out the pairs of words that can be replaced with a contraction. Write the contraction above the words.

Hughes to Become Youngest Astronaut

    Jasmine Hughes is only nine
years old. ~~She will~~ (She'll) be the first child
to journey into space. Jasmine has
been training since she was four.
~~She will~~ (She'll) travel on the space shuttle
Investigator. Six other astronauts
will be in her crew. ~~They will~~ (They'll) have to
work well as a team. Darren Unger

will be the commander. ~~He will~~ (He'll) be
the leader of the crew. They know
their mission is important. ~~It will~~ (It'll) help
scientists learn more about the
universe. The world will be able to
watch the trip on TV. ~~We will~~ (We'll) see
history being made!

page 125

Answer Key

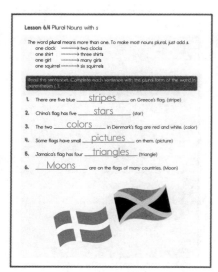

page 126

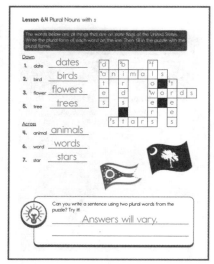

page 127

page 128

page 129

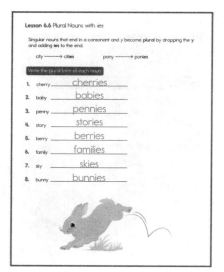

page 130

page 131

Answer Key

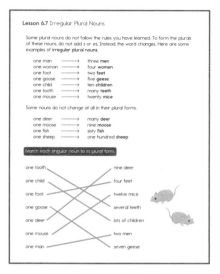

page 132

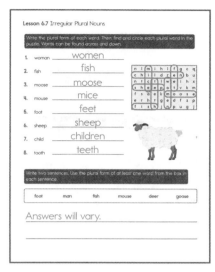

page 133

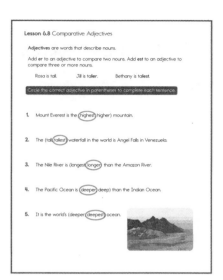

page 134

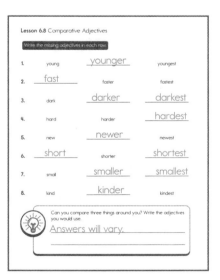

page 135

page 136

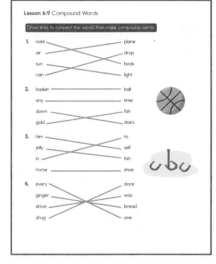

page 137

Answer Key

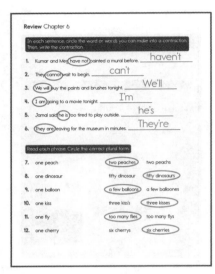

page 138

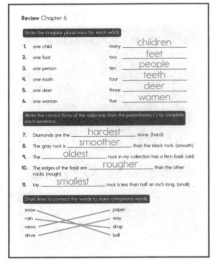

page 139

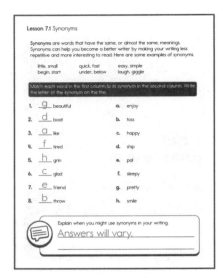

page 142

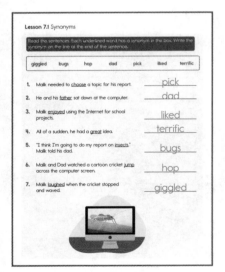

page 143

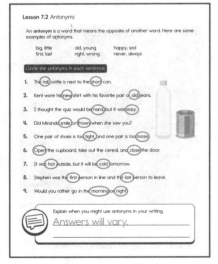

page 144

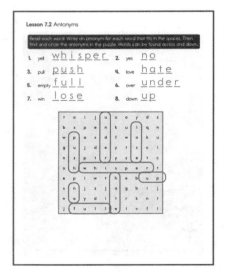

page 145

Spectrum Language Arts **Grade 2**

Answer Key

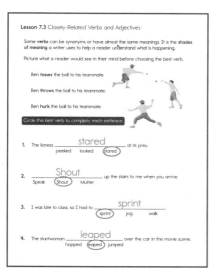

page 146

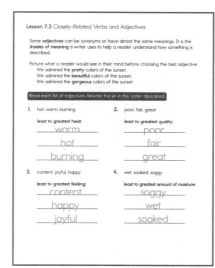

page 147

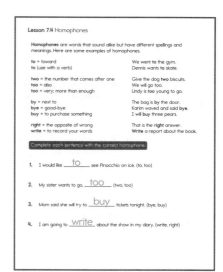

page 148

page 149

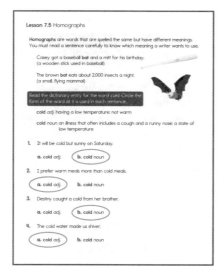

page 150

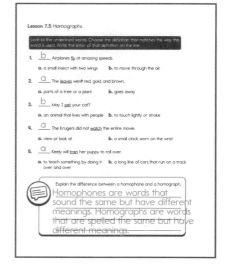

page 151

Answer Key

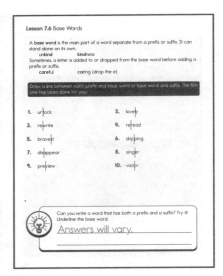

Lesson 7.6 Base Words

A **base word** is the main part of a word separate from a prefix or suffix. It can stand alone on its own.
unkind   **kindness**
Sometimes, a letter is added to or dropped from the base word before adding a prefix or suffix.
careful   **caring (drop the e)**

Draw a line between each prefix and base word or base word and suffix. The first one has been done for you.

1. un|lock   2. love|ly
3. re|write   4. re|read
5. brave|st   6. skip|ping
7. dis|appear   8. sing|er
9. pre|view   10. visit|or

Can you write a word that has both a prefix and a suffix? Try it! Underline the base word.
Answers will vary.

page 152

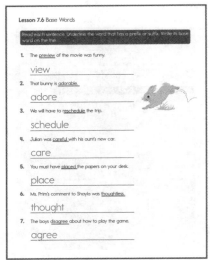

Lesson 7.6 Base Words

Read each sentence. Underline the word that has a prefix or suffix. Write its base word on the line.

1. The preview of the movie was funny.
view
2. That bunny is adorable.
adore
3. We will have to reschedule the trip.
schedule
4. Julian is careful with his aunt's new car.
care
5. You must have placed the papers on your desk.
place
6. Ms. Prim's comment to Shayla was thoughtless.
thought
7. The boys disagree about how to play the game.
agree

page 153

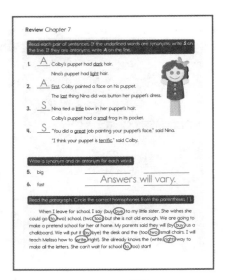

Review Chapter 7

Read each pair of sentences. If the underlined words are synonyms, write **S** on the line. If they are antonyms, write **A** on the line.

1. **A** Colby's puppet had dark hair.
Nina's puppet had light hair.
2. **A** First, Colby painted a face on his puppet.
The last thing Nina did was button her puppet's dress.
3. **S** Nina tied a little bow in her puppet's hair.
Colby's puppet had a small frog in its pocket.
4. **S** "You did a great job painting your puppet's face," said Nina.
"I think your puppet is terrific," said Colby.

Write a synonym and an antonym for each word.

5. big
6. fast   **Answers will vary.**

Read the paragraph. Circle the correct homophones from the parentheses ( ).

When I leave for school, I say (buy, bye) to my little sister. She wishes she could go (to, two) school, (two, too) but she is not old enough. We are going to make a pretend school for her at home. My parents said they will (by, buy) us a chalkboard. We will put it (by, bye) the desk and the (too, two) small chairs. I will teach Melissa how to (write, right). She already knows the (write, right) way to make all the letters. She can't wait for school (to, too) start!

page 154

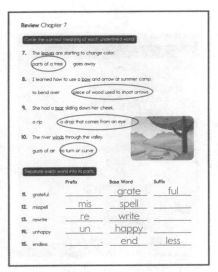

Review Chapter 7

Circle the correct meaning of each underlined word.

7. The leaves are starting to change color.
(parts of a tree)   goes away
8. I learned how to use a bow and arrow at summer camp.
to bend over   (piece of wood used to shoot arrows)
9. She had a tear sliding down her cheek.
a rip   (a drop that comes from an eye)
10. The river winds through the valley.
gusts of air   (to turn or curve)

Separate each word into its parts.

	Prefix	Base Word	Suffix
11. grateful		grate	ful
12. misspell	mis	spell	
13. rewrite	re	write	
14. unhappy	un	happy	
15. endless		end	less

page 155

Learning Checkpoint Chapters 5–7

Circle the verb in each sentence. If it is correct, write a ✓ on the line. If it is not correct, write the correct form of the verb on the line.

1. I likes camping.   **like**
2. We roast marshmallows on the fire.   ✓
3. My sister tell a scary story.   **tells**
4. I ask for a funny one!   ✓

Circle the correct verb to complete each sentence.

5. I (is, am) excited to go hiking.
6. Do you (has, have) your backpack ready?

Rewrite each sentence in the past tense.

7. I hike in Yellowstone National Park.
I hiked in Yellowstone National Park.
8. It is the first national park in the US.
It was the first national park in the US.

page 156

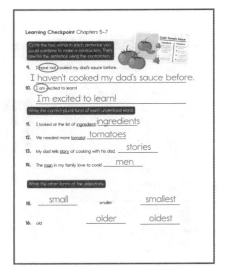

Learning Checkpoint Chapters 5–7

Circle the two words in each sentence you could combine to make a contraction. Then, rewrite the sentence using the contraction.

9. I have not cooked my dad's sauce before.
I haven't cooked my dad's sauce before.
10. I am excited to learn!
I'm excited to learn!

Write the correct plural form of each underlined word.

11. I looked at the list of ingredient.   **ingredients**
12. We needed more tomato!   **tomatoes**
13. My dad tells story of cooking with his dad.   **stories**
14. The man in my family love to cook!   **men**

Write the other forms of the adjectives.

15. **small**   smaller   **smallest**
16. old   **older**   **oldest**

page 157

Spectrum Language Arts **Grade 2**

Answer Key

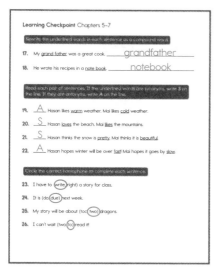

Learning Checkpoint Chapters 5–7

Rewrite the underlined words in each sentence as a compound word.

17. My grand father was a great cook. **grandfather**
18. He wrote his recipes in a note book. **notebook**

Read each pair of sentences. If the underlined words are synonyms, write S on the line. If they are antonyms, write A on the line.

19. **A** Hasan likes warm weather. Mai likes cold weather.
20. **S** Hasan loves the beach. Mai likes the mountains.
21. **S** Hasan thinks the snow is pretty. Mai thinks it is beautiful.
22. **A** Hasan hopes winter will be over fast! Mai hopes it goes by slow.

Circle the correct homophone to complete each sentence.

23. I have to (write)/right) a story for class.
24. It is (do/(due)) next week.
25. My story will be about (too/(two)) dragons.
26. I can't wait (two/(to)) read it!

page 158

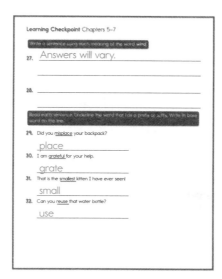

Learning Checkpoint Chapters 5–7

Write a sentence using each meaning of the word wind.

27. _Answers will vary._
28. _____

Read each sentence. Underline the word that has a prefix or suffix. Write its base word on the line.

29. Did you misplace your backpack? **place**
30. I am grateful for your help. **grate**
31. That is the smallest kitten I have ever seen! **small**
32. Can you reuse that water bottle? **use**

page 159

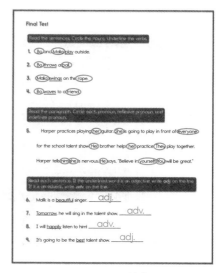

Final Test

Read the sentences. Circle the nouns. Underline the verbs.

1. (Bo) and (Malia) play outside.
2. (Bo) throws a (ball).
3. (Malia) swings on the (rope).
4. (Bo) waves to a (friend).

Read the paragraph. Circle each pronoun, reflexive pronoun, and indefinite pronoun.

5. Harper practices playing (her) guitar. (She) is going to play in front of (everyone) for the school talent show. (Her) brother helps (her) practice. (They) play together. Harper tells (him) (she) is nervous. (He) says, "Believe in (yourself.) (You) will be great."

Read each sentence. If the underlined word is an adjective, write adj. on the line. If it is an adverb, write adv. on the line.

6. Malik is a beautiful singer. **adj.**
7. Tomorrow, he will sing in the talent show. **adv.**
8. I will happily listen to him! **adv.**
9. It's going to be the best talent show. **adj.**

page 160

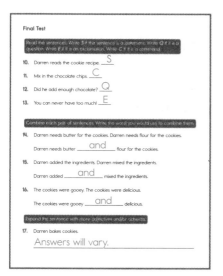

Final Test

Read the sentences. Write S if the sentence is a statement. Write Q if it is a question. Write E if it is an exclamation. Write C if it is a command.

10. Darren reads the cookie recipe. **S**
11. Mix in the chocolate chips. **C**
12. Did he add enough chocolate? **Q**
13. You can never have too much! **E**

Combine each pair of sentences. Write the word you would use to combine them.

14. Darren needs butter for the cookies. Darren needs flour for the cookies.
Darren needs butter **and** flour for the cookies.
15. Darren added the ingredients. Darren mixed the ingredients.
Darren added **and** mixed the ingredients.
16. The cookies were gooey. The cookies were delicious.
The cookies were gooey **and** delicious.

Expand the sentence with more adjectives and/or adverbs.

17. Darren bakes cookies.
Answers will vary.

page 161

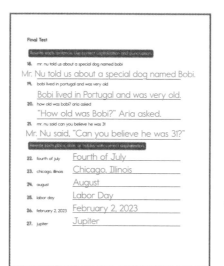

Final Test

Rewrite each sentence. Use correct capitalization and punctuation.

18. mr. nu told us about a special dog named bobi
Mr. Nu told us about a special dog named Bobi.
19. bobi lived in portugal and was very old
Bobi lived in Portugal and was very old.
20. how old was bobi? aria asked
"How old was Bobi?" Aria asked.
21. mr. nu said can you believe he was 31
Mr. Nu said, "Can you believe he was 31?"

Rewrite each place, date, or holiday with correct capitalization.

22. fourth of july **Fourth of July**
23. chicago, illinois **Chicago, Illinois**
24. august **August**
25. labor day **Labor Day**
26. february 2, 2023 **February 2, 2023**
27. jupiter **Jupiter**

page 162

Final Test

Rewrite each phrase as a possessive.

28. the tail of the cat **the cat's tail**
29. the eyes of the boy **the boy's eyes**
30. the shell of a turtle **the turtle's shell**
31. the wheel of a car **the car's wheel**

Rewrite each phrase. Use an abbreviation in place of the underlined word.

32. Monday, July 14 **Mon., July 14**
33. Doctor Sanchez **Dr. Sanchez**
34. Mister Taylor **Mr. Taylor**
35. January 1 **Jan. 1**

Rewrite each sentence. Add commas where they are needed.

36. Dad is going to the store but he has to write a list first.
Dad is going to the store, but he has to write a list first.
37. We need bread fruit and peanut butter.
We need bread, fruit, and peanut butter.
38. The grocery store is in Portland Maine.
The grocery store is in Portland, Maine.

page 163

Answer Key

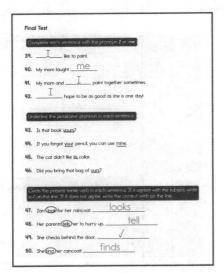

Final Test

Complete each sentence with the pronoun *I* or *me*.

39. __I__ like to paint.

40. My mom taught __me__

41. My mom and __I__ paint together sometimes.

42. __I__ hope to be as good as she is one day!

Underline the possessive pronoun in each sentence.

43. Is that book <u>yours</u>?

44. If you forgot <u>your</u> pencil, you can use <u>mine</u>.

45. The cat didn't like <u>its</u> collar.

46. Did you bring that bag of <u>ours</u>?

Circle the present tense verb in each sentence. If it agrees with the subject, write a ✓ on the line. If it does not agrees, write the correct verb on the line.

47. Zara ⟨looks⟩ for her raincoat. __looks__

48. Her parents ⟨tell⟩ her to hurry up. __tell__

49. She checks behind the door. __✓__

50. She ⟨find⟩ her raincoat! __finds__

page 164

Final Test

Complete each sentence with the correct past tense form of the verb in parentheses ( ).

51. Maya Angelou __was__ an excellent writer. (is, was)

52. She __wrote__ books and poems. (wrote, writes)

53. Maya __broke__ records and made history. (breaks, broke)

54. She __had__ a great mind! (has, had)

Read the paragraph. Complete each sentence with the plural form of the word in parentheses ( ).

55. We spotted __dolphins__ (dolphin) out in the water. A

bunch of __families__ (family) gathered to see. My sister told

me they blow __bubbles__ (bubble). It helps them catch

__fish__ (fish) to eat! We jumped in the

__waves__ (wave). My sister splashed me. She said she was

pretending to use her __fins__ (fin)!

page 165

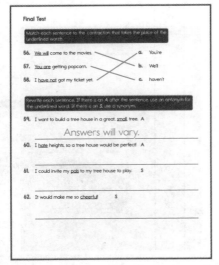

Final Test

Match each sentence to the contraction that takes the place of the underlined words.

56. <u>We will</u> come to the movies.   a. You're

57. <u>You are</u> getting popcorn.   b. We'll

58. I <u>have not</u> got my ticket yet.   c. haven't

Rewrite each sentence. If there is an *A* after the sentence, use an antonym for the underlined word. If there is an *S*, use a synonym.

59. I want to build a tree house in a great, <u>small</u> tree. A

__Answers will vary.__

60. I <u>hate</u> heights, so a tree house would be perfect! A

61. I could invite my <u>pals</u> to my tree house to play.   S

62. It would make me so <u>cheerful!</u>   S

page 166

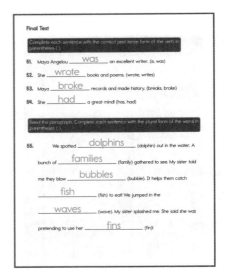

Final Test

For each word, write its base word on the line.

63. redo __do__   64. displease __please__

65. teacher __teach__   66. untie __tie__

67. cutest __cute__   68. pretest __test__

Write a sentence for each homophone: *to, too,* and *two.*

69. ____

__Answers will vary.__

70. ____

71. ____

page 167